ANDREW NICKOLDS

GATE GATE

THE SHATTERING LID-LIFTER THAT KILLS ALL KNOWN CONSPIRACY THEORIES... DEAD!

Illustrated by
David Austin, Nick Newman and Kipper Williams

PAN BOOKS
LONDON, SYDNEY & AUCKLAND

First published 1993 by Pan Macmillan Limited

a division of Pan Macmillan Publishers Limited
Cavaye Place London SW10 9PG
and Basingstoke

Associated companies throughout the world

ISBN 0 330 33204 X

Copyright © Andrew Nickolds and Richard Stoneman 1993

Illustrations copyright © David Austin, Nick Newman
and Kipper Williams 1993

The right of Andrew Nickolds and Richard Stoneman
to be identified as the authors of this work has been
asserted by them in accordance with the Copyright,
Designs and Patents Act 1988.

All rights reserved. No reproduction, copy or transmission
of this publication may be made without written permission.
No paragraph of this publication may be reproduced, copied or
transmitted save with written permission or in accordance with
the provisions of the Copyright Act 1956 (as amended). Any
person who does any unauthorised act in relation to
this publication may be liable to criminal prosecution
and civil claims for damages.

1 3 5 7 9 8 6 4 2

A CIP catalogue record for this book is available from
the British Library

Typeset by Pan Macmillan Limited
Printed by Cox & Wyman Ltd., Reading, Berks

This book is sold subject to the condition that it shall not,
by way of trade or otherwise, be lent, re-sold, hired out,
or otherwise circulated without the publisher's prior consent
in any form of binding or cover other than that in which
it is published and without a similar condition including this
condition being imposed on the subsequent purchaser

CONTENTS

INTRODUCTION
THE GREAT GATE CONUNDRUM
1

HAWKING-GATE 5
APPLEGATE 10
ARKGATE 14
WATERGATE 18
JERICHOGATE 22
GARDENGATE 28
GRAILGATE 34
FORESTGATE 38
ARROWGATE 41
POKERGATE 47
BARDGATE 52
TRAITOR'S GATE 57
ALDGATE 62
NAVIGATE 66
BRANDENBURG-GATE 73
SUFFRAGATE 78
FATTYGATE 85
HARROGATE 88
ABDIGATE 97
LAMPPOSTGATE 102
LILLIBETGATE 104
HOOVERGATE 112
CROP CIRCLES GATE 118
MILLERGATE 123
THATCHERGATE 130

CONCLUSIONS
135

STARTING-GATE 137

INTRODUCTION
THE GREAT GATE CONUNDRUM

> 'All great events in world history reappear in one fashion or another – the first time as tragedy, the second as farce.'
>
> Karl Marx

Our quest could not have begun more mundanely. It was a grey autumn morning in 1992 – it is worth recording the circumstances exactly, in view of the enormous distances, in both Earth miles and the realm of the imagination, we were to travel on our voyage of discovery.

We had almost finished reading the newspapers. The gas man had just been to read the meter and we had talked loudly about plans to spend the evening with our respective partners, to show him we were straight. Strange to think now, after both our relationships disintegrated under the pressure of compiling this book! And how closed our minds must have been!

Anyway, Robert the gas man had gone and we sat thinking of ways to avoid starting to write. It occurred to us simultaneously that there was something curious in the newspapers, broadsheet and tabloid alike. A preoccupation with the word 'Gate'. That day alone had seen references to 'Camillagate', 'Threshergate' and 'Squidgygate': apparently innocent – if somewhat lazy – shorthand for alleged scandals involving the Great and the Good (and not-so-Good!).

But *was* it as innocent as that? Why *had* the country's journalists suddenly latched on to this supposedly humdrum suffix? Was it merely one of those evanescent phrases that

INTRODUCTION

become famous for the equivalent of fifteen minutes (like 'catering manageress', 'bulimia', 'Tampax' and 'bastard') before disappearing? Or did it represent anything more sinister? Could the press have been privy to something denied to the general public, an arcane secret too explosive to reveal except in this most cryptic of terms?

The answer, on the face of it, was no. But we weren't prepared to leave it at that. After all, imagine if some of our distinguished predecessors in the investigative field had, instead of exploring the village of Rennes-le-Château, opted for a pleasant lunch of *moules-et-frites*. The world would never have heard the true story of how our Lord Jesus Christ was smuggled out of the Holy Land by his wife and children, and spent his last years in happy retirement in Dundogoodin, a village in the south of France!

The more we thought about it, the more possible it appeared that there just might be some interconnected pattern to history, its great events and scandals, and that the codeword 'Gate' could be the key to the door.

We decided to start our researches with what we thought was the first recorded instance of the phenomenon: 'Watergate'. Our thinking was right, but in our simplistic assumption of the circumstances and the date (the attempted cover-up of a break-in at the Democratic Headquarters in 1972) we could hardly have been more wrong!

Months of searching through dusty tomes in some of the world's most esoteric libraries, and deciphering the words of learned men through the ages, eventually led us to a small Provençal town that for security's sake we had better call 'X'.

There, in an underground chamber in 'X'-en-Provence, after moving the Ark of the Covenant to one side, we found secreted behind a wall what have since become known to scholars as the 'Red Sea Scrolls'. Anyone who can't wait to read the *real* facts behind Moses's leading the Israelites in their Exodus from Egypt (in what, were one to be facetious, one

INTRODUCTION

might call 'History's First *Un*cover-Up') should turn to page 18.

This first 'Watergate' was only the beginning: we were on our way. Time and again, our researches and discoveries were to prove the truth of Marx's dictum: that there is literally nothing new under the sun. What's more, the 'official' version of history is usually nothing more than a barrier put across the road of truth, and manned by shadowy figures desperate that the seeker after the facts should go no further. But we say this to Messrs Vested Interests PLC: we're on to you! That we have stumbled across the conspiracy theory to end them all is in our opinion beyond doubt.

There will be people who accuse us of conducting a kind of 'wild Gate chase' through history. To this we plead Not Guilty: though the conclusions we draw are open to question, we are convinced that they could possibly constitute – in our humble submission – the most shattering secret of the last three million years.

A. N.
R. C. S.

Oddbins, Rockall.
May, 1993.

HAWKING-GATE

To discover if there was anything not quite kosher about the creation of the Universe we turned first, like millions of readers before us, to Professor Stephen Hawking's famous book *A Brief History of Time*. On page 9 (the number is important) we found the following statement:

> 'One could imagine that God created the
> Universe at the instant of the Big Bang . . .'

Several questions immediately sprang to mind about this extremely – as we saw it – convenient explosion:

WHO HEARD IT?

HOW DO WE KNOW IT WAS A BANG?

HOW DO WE KNOW THERE WAS ONLY ONE?

Naturally we were expecting some answers from the Cambridge savant. But instead we were engulfed by a phenomenon of even greater mystery, best summed up thus:

IT IS IMPOSSIBLE TO READ BEYOND PAGE 17
OF *'A BRIEF HISTORY OF TIME'*.

Everybody we asked who had bought the book over the years told us of the same experience. Public libraries corroborated our suspicions: examination of the copies on their shelves revealed the grey line of finger-marks down the edge of the book . . . *but only up to page 17*. The rest was virgin white!

HAWKING-GATE

Moreover, the time taken to reach that point in the book is in inverse proportion to the energy expended in doing something else instead, as this diagram shows:

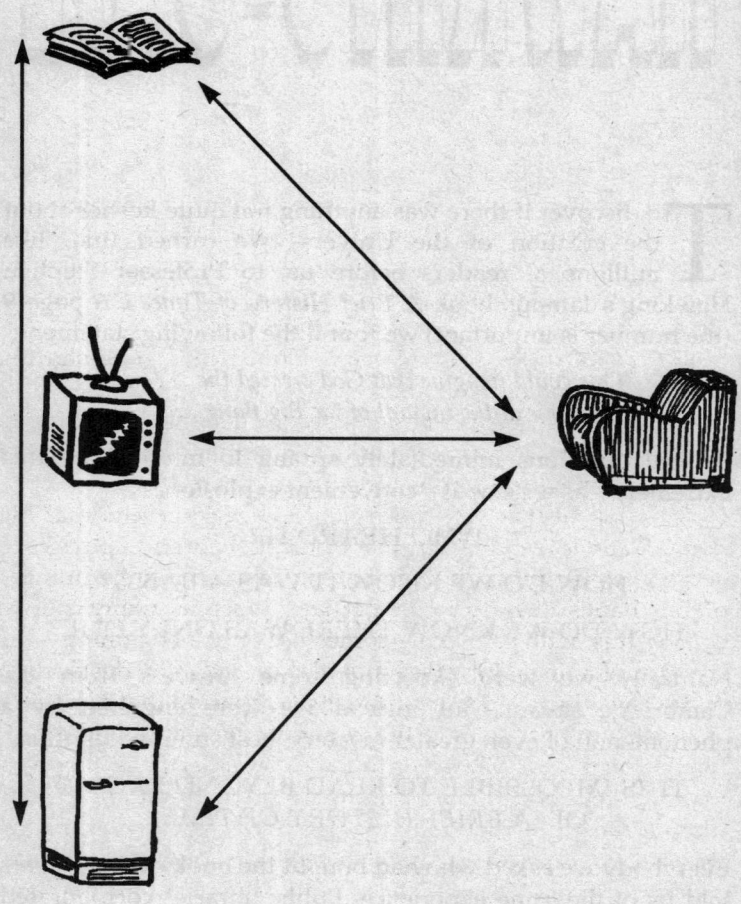

Diagram showing relationship between armchair, book, TV set and fridge, and routes thereto.

HAWKING-GATE

Could it be that Hawking *had* stumbled on the answer to the chicken-and-egg riddle of God and the Universe? And that greater forces – the 'powers that may or may not be' – were at work, preventing anybody else from finding out?

What follows is, of course, supposition. But can anyone disprove it?

In 1781 Immanuel Kant published his *Critique of Pure Reason*, in which he questioned whether the Universe had a beginning in time. (Despite the book being in *Die Sontag Zeit's* best-seller list for three and a half years, his line of thought led to rival philosophers nicknaming the author 'Stupid' Kant.)

For our purposes, however, the *Critique* is a good starting point for opening up the debate.

For why *should* there, of necessity, be a single beginning to time and space? Why not several 'beginnings' – fresh starts, if you like – with none of them identifiable as the 'first'?

A notion of this kind does not, however, preclude a 'Big Bang'. Rather, it widens the black hole of theoretical physics to admit the possibility of there having been an infinite number of Big Bangs already, with perhaps twice as many still to come. Thus, with each Bang comes not only a beginning – the creation of a new Universe – but also an *end* – the destruction of the one which had been in existence up until that moment.

If one now brings into the equation the 'cause and effect' requirement, it can be seen that a *multiple* Big Bang theory is logically superior to, and therefore more conjecturally viable than, the *single* Big Bang theory. For *we* can say that each Bang must have been caused by something (nuclear warfare, human error at a power station, a build-up of bovine methane in an abattoir) but those who say the world had just one beginning cannot name any cause of the Big Bang because anything *happening* before anything was *created* is logically 'meaningless' (whatever – as Professor Hawking would say – that means).

The notion of an expanding Universe is easily accommodated within our theory, albeit in a different guise. For the Universe can certainly grow *in between Bangs*, but it must also shrink to nothing *as a result of* each Bang. Thus, perhaps we should talk rather in terms of an 'inflatable' Universe, capable of being 'deflated' and stored in a location with a phase space of zero.

But enough of space – what of *time*?

Professor Hawking's *Brief History* might suggest to the reader that time can go backwards as well as forwards (note how the eye is drawn *back* over the final paragraph of page 17 again and again) but why should a direction be ascribed to this concept at all? With the Multiple Bang theory the mystery surrounding – and therefore the speculation about – travelling 'back' in time disappears. Instead there is the certain knowledge that each event being experienced has already been experienced by someone in a previous inter–Bang period. For if there is nothing in the Universe at the moment of each new creation, it follows logically that the growth – the formation – of each fresh Universe will replicate, to a greater or lesser extent, the growth of the one before that. Or at least, there is no reason why it should not.

If this theory of ours was to take its place in the academy of good ideas (alongside gravity, $E = mc^2$ and ring-pull cans) we knew we would have to show the doubting Stephens of this world some 'proof'. We therefore set about searching for clues in the earliest historical record to hand – the so-called 'Bible'.

INTERESTING FOOTNOTE

We rang Professor 'Keep Talking' Hawking for his comments on our theory. In fact we rang many times over a six-month period, at all hours of the day and night. All we ever got was the identical, repetitive monotone of an answering machine (even when we had first checked with his neighbours that the Professor was at home!). Proof enough in our view that the Professor knows something he doesn't want the rest of the world to find out . . . or had he been got at by someone? And if so . . . *who*?

AppleGate
OR
Would You Adam-and-Eve it?

First we decided to investigate the man and woman from whom we are all supposedly descended, to see if there was any substance in the saying 'Two's company: three, you've got a conspiracy'.

On the face of it they were the perfect couple. Adam had been fashioned by God out of the living clay, and Eve from Adam's rib. Neither had had previous relationships. They lived across the Garden of Eden from each other, saw each other when they needed to, shared meals. Adam looked with benign tolerance on Eve's love of the beasts of the field and her eagerness to adopt any of the fowls of the air that suffered injury. Then the Serpent came between them.

Or did it?

The Bible relates that the Serpent seduced Eve into eating the forbidden fruit from the Tree of Knowledge, whereupon she and Adam became ashamed of their nakedness and hid from God. Yet it must be remembered that, in common with most Old Testament stories, the Bible's is just one of several versions.

Many of the Hebrew beliefs that have been handed down for centuries were adapted from earlier sources, in particular the *Babylonian Genesis* – or as it is better known now, since the film rights were snapped up, the *Hollywood Babylonian Genesis*.

Controversially, this version lays the blame for this very

first 'Gate' squarely on the shoulders of Adam. Eve had discovered him drawing lewd clothed pictures of the Serpent in a cave, and tells God. God confronts Adam. What follows is a free translation of the subsequent 'trial' as reported in the scriptures.

GOD: Are you now, or have you ever been, in a sexual relationship with that serpent?

ADAM: Come on. Eve's adopted the guy. That'd be like laying down with my own daughter.

GOD: How would you know? I haven't yet made your loins fruitful.

ADAM: Oh yeah, I forgot. That day you were out creating the Land of Nod. When can we expect the access road?

EVE: Maybe God would like to rest from his labours, if you'd just give him a minute.

ADAM: Excuse me for breathing. Excuse me for donating a spare rib for the betterment of mankind. That was one of a set.
EVE: You did OK. Who was it who was made in God's own image?
ADAM: Sure. Glasses. What were the rejects like?
GOD: If we could just get back to the Tree of Knowledge.
ADAM: She's making it up. She's crazy. What do I want with fruit? I gotta barbecue, don't I?
EVE: Murderer!
ADAM: Hey, wake up and smell the coffee! This is nature, right? Red in tooth and claw. By the way, I got a question.
GOD: What?
ADAM: Why am I in the country? I *hate* the country!
GOD: I have given thee paradise on earth, and . . .
ADAM: And the rest. Bugs. Why couldn't you save them till last and spend a little energy giving us a decent deli?
EVE: First chance I get I'm giving my side of the story to the Good Jews Bible.
ADAM: Hear that? If she had a mother, that's what she'd sound like. Just goes to show: you can take the Girl out of the Garden but you can't take the Garden out of the Girl.
GOD: QUIET!
ADAM: Sez who?
GOD: The Supreme Being. The Alpha and Omega. Maker of All Things.
ADAM: Yeah? Eat my shorts.
EVE: He's been like this ever since he started wearing them. He's sick in the head. He tried to put me in therapy and all I did was give a good home to poor Serpy.
ADAM: Serpy. Jeez. Fruitcake. The defence rests.
EVE: At least I'm not a pervert. [TO GOD] He wanted to know what it was like having a coil!
ADAM: Hey, *I'm* talking to the Big Guy. [TO GOD] Anyway, how do I know you exist? And if so, who created *you*, OK? Like the man said – which came first, the Chicken McNugget or the Egg McMuffin?

GOD: Enough, already. This is my verdict. I will put enmity between thee and the woman . . .
ADAM: We got that, bub. That ship has sailed.
GOD: Shut up. And between thy seed and her seed; it shall bruise thy head, and thou shalt bruise his heel.
ADAM: He would say that, wouldn't He?
EVE: What about the serpent?
GOD: I was coming to that. Serpent, upon thy belly shalt thou go, and . . .
ADAM & EVE: No, no – who gets custody?

ARKGATE

We were digging for dirt on Adolf Hitler in the newspaper library when one of us communicated to the other that no press cuttings could be found. Silence is the golden rule at

The Ararat Argus
DATE: A LONG, LONG TIME AGO

NOAH NO MORE
End of an 'ero!

Our proprietor, Noah, has died at the age of nine hundred and fifty. We salute a great man and look back on his past achievements.

Born the son of Lamech, he changed his name a number of times before finally settling on Noah. And yet it is as 'Captain No' that he'll best be remembered. That nickname first came into use after the great flood three hundred and fifty years ago, when Noah turned down thousands of requests from sinners to join him and his family on board his luxury Ark *No 'Er Indoors* (named after his beloved wife). At one point on the voyage it was thought that Noah had fallen through a gap in the railings into the waters below, but this proved a false alarm and the drowning victim was later found to be a mammoth (now extinct).

A confidant of the world's most senior statesmen, it was said

ARKGATE

Colindale so a note was passed from one to the other with "No AH" written on it. The scribble was on a library request slip, however, and was left at our regular table overnight. Imagine our surprise the next morning to find the first known reference to NOAH awaiting us in photocopy form (together with an illustration from *Arking Monthly*).

---

that Noah 'found grace in the eyes of the Lord',[1] and he was often seen walking with God. Perhaps that explains the extraordinary, exclusive covenant his lawyers negotiated with the Lord, after long protracted meetings in the penthouse conference room of Noah House. The signing was celebrated with a huge rainbow display and barbecue of burnt offerings. The power this covenant gave to Noah allowed him to take on the chisel unions . . . and win! There can be no doubt that without Noah, the 'Grey 'Un' would still be produced by the labour-intensive, cold stone method.

With instructions from God to multiply, Noah did just that, floating the Ararat News Group a year after the flood ended and adding thousands of private companies to his Noah Communications Corporation. He was a great internationalist and published *The Middle-Easterner* more as an act of faith than as a going business concern.

His decision to purchase Ararat United was indicative of his love of sport and the frequent pre-match appearances on the pitch of 'The Big Floater', as the United fans used to call him, will be sorely missed.

Noah leaves a wife and three sons. We pay tribute to someone once described as 'a just man and perfect in his generations'.[2] Amen to that!

1. Editor's Note: see The Bible – Genesis 6.8
2. Editor's Note: see The Bible – Genesis 6.9

ARKGATE

The Ararat Argus
DATE: A LONG TIME AGO

GOOD RIDDANCE YOU FAT BASTARD
Noah was a crook!

We can exclusively reveal that the former owner of the *Ararat Argus*, Noah (or 'Captain No Scruples' to you and me), was an embezzling fraudster who should have been drowned at birth.

Thousands of dumb creatures are today facing a future without hope. Having duped them to join him on his Ark for the great flood (or 'Black Forty Days and Forty Nights' as it is now called), the late, unlamented Noah spent the next three and a half centuries selling each beast, fowl and fish down the river – as food for mankind The unlucky couples who signed up for the procreation exercise were promised the earth but it was Noah's troubled communications empire which profited from their lives, and now every moving thing has nothing to look forward to but providing a square meal for one of Noah's descendants.

The greatest scandal since Creation first came to light after rumours started circulating that Noah had been found naked, drunk and unconscious in a tent, straight after the Flood.[3] Suggestions that his life had not been as unimpeachable as we had previously reported were quickly followed up by our reporters, and we have to confess – HE FOOLED US TOO!

ARKGATE

The Ararat News Group is in turmoil tonight as we try to do what we can to honour the promises made to all the beasts concerned. Control of the Communications Corporation has shifted to Noah's sons Shem and Japheth. The youngest son, Ham, has been frozen out of the family business after it became clear that he was the source of the story about his father's alcohol dependency.[4] Faced yesterday with a string of difficult questions from a hastily convened House of the Lord Select Committee, Shem and Japheth refused to say anything about Noah's business practices. Speaking through their lawyers, they claimed that any comment at this stage might prejudice their case before the Highest Judge Of All.

An auction of Noah's possessions and property – notably the Ark and his impressive vineyard – is expected to take place in the near future.

Sorry, folks – but at least we now know who put the RAT in ARARAT!

3. Editor's Note: see The Bible – Genesis 9.21
4. Editor's Note: see The Bible – Genesis 9.22

How unlike our own Secret Intelligence Service is the Israeli version – Mossad. There are no secrets in the Promised Land and spies are actively encouraged to write their memoirs after retiring. Popular autobiographies in the book shops of Tel Aviv include *This Climate You Call Treason?* and *Spycatcher, Shmycatcher*. Requests to see the file of any known Israeli are welcomed by Mossad's courteous telephone sales staff who faxed us the following report on MOSES within minutes of our call.

TOP SECRET – FOR THINE EYES ONLY

MEMORANDUM

To: M[1]
From: AHV[2]
Date: 3rd Kislev 1137 BC

Re: MOSES

1. I have now completed my preliminary investigation into Moses and must warn you that there are grounds for believing that he was – as suggested by DHD[3] in his memorandum dated 24th Ab 1138 – working for the

1. Head of Mossad
2. Acting Head of V Section - in charge of personnel
3. Deputy Head of D Section - dealing with all Middle East activity

WATERGATE

Egyptians throughout his service with this department. There are a number of events and circumstances which lead me to this conclusion. Naturally, you will wish to discuss at a later stage how our positive vetting procedures can be tightened to prevent any further threats to the credibility of our department by revelations of this kind. I shall limit myself merely to reporting the facts.

2. I have found proof that Moses was not, after all, brought up by his parents, Mr and Mrs Levi. Apparently, there was an informal adoption of Moses by an Egyptian – the daughter of a Pharaoh no less – when he was just a few days old. This early contact with the lifestyle of prominent Egyptians must have played an important part in shaping his attitude towards their country, and towards ours.

3. At university in Alexandria, he fell into company with a group of pro-Egyptians called 'the Apostles'. He was active in the University's debating society and frequently spoke out in favour of Pharaohism. (No record of this behaviour had reached V Section at the time of his recruitment.)

4. Moses first came to the department's notice after an incident when he saw an Egyptian fighting with an Hebrew. Moses apparently assassinated the Egyptian with an impressive display of controlled aggression. (Although we must now ask whether this was in fact a set-up: was it really an Hebrew and did the Egyptian actually die?)

5. After fleeing to Sinai, Moses was recruited by the department and given a cover job as a shepherd, allowing him to travel widely and report on any unusual mountaintop activity. We now know that by this stage he

WATERGATE

was working for the Egyptians. Tablets in Moses' own hand have been found in a booby-trapped Ark (defused and dismantled by T(S)[4]) which reveal details of a conversation he had with his Egyptian contact (codenamed 'Burning Bush') at Horeb. 'Burning Bush' equipped Moses with a concealed weapon (the deadly Snake-stick much favoured at that time by Egyptian special forces) and briefed him on how to implement a campaign of disinformation against Israel.

6. I am of the firm opinion that alarm bells should have been ringing somewhere in the department when Moses gained direct access to the Pharaoh. To be allowed to plead for the release of the Israelites _in person_ seems, in hindsight, a clear indication that Moses had unreasonable influence within the Egyptian hierarchy and I find it extraordinary that this lapse in his cover was not spotted by someone in the department at that time.

7. The stories of plagues affecting the people of Egypt must now be disregarded since it was Moses himself who informed the department about them. And the departure of the Israelites from Egypt (Operation Exodus) was certainly _not_ the perilous journey he claimed (cf. Transportation Report No. 3788/M/3). The Egyptians clearly wanted Moses to escape so that he could do their work and the suggestion that the Red Sea parted to allow the Israelites to walk across is so absurd that I find it difficult to believe this explanation was accepted at the departmental debrief. A map found with the Tablets (cf. para 5 above) shows that Moses followed a path to the Dead Sea where he and his followers simply floated across the water. There was no need for the Egyptians to keep up the pretence of pursuing the

---

4. Technical Support Section - explosives experts

WATERGATE

Israelites after that point and they gave the impression that the 'chase' was over by feigning death by drowning.

8. I am also surprised that the disappearance of Moses for forty days and forty nights at Mount Sinai did not arouse suspicion. It seems clear that he must have spent that period with 'Burning Bush', being briefed on what disinformation to give to the Israelites. We now know that the main planks of that disinformation - 'The Ten Commandments' - should be disregarded. So too must the books of Leviticus, Numbers and Deuteronomy. The design fault in the Tabernacles must be blamed on Moses and I think we should feel lucky that only three thousand Israelites were killed by the Levites at the Golden Calf riots - if Moses had been more successful in stirring up civil unrest the number could have been doubled.

9. It is now obvious why Moses did not enter the Promised Land with the rest of the Israelites: he was about to defect. I suggest that, rather than dying at Mount Nebo, Moses is alive and well and living in Egypt.

10. This is clearly highly embarrassing for the department. Other countries will be reluctant to share intelligence with us if any of the above leaks out. I can at least reassure you that rumours of Caleb and Joshua also having been in the pay of the Egyptians are without foundation. And talk of a so-called 'Fourth Man' is nonsense.

<u>AHV</u>

JERICHOGATE

The microfiche system at Company House in London lists firms which have gone bust in chronological order. The first recorded business to cease trading was therefore easily identified as Miraculous Tubing of Sheffield. Close inspection of their thin (and ancient) file revealed the yellowed, barely legible facsimiles of terse supply orders, and a mysterious design for what appears to be a primitive weapon.

To: Miraculous Tubing, Sheffield, England
From: Joshua Demolition Co, nr Jericho, Canaan
Date: 1st Tishri 1242 BC

Understand you have experimented with prototype of ram's horn trumpet. Wish to purchase large quantity of precision-tooled tubing and suspect ram's horn ideal material for our purposes. Please inform if willing to supply goods on receipt of blueprints (to follow by courier).

Achan
Marketing Director


```
To: Joshua Demolition Co
From: Miraculous Tubing
Date: 24th Adar 1241 BC
```

In receipt of blueprints. Understand seven inter-connecting parts of tubing required, ranging from 2 cubits diameter to 1.75 reeds.

JERICHOGATE

Must ask for purpose of product before supplying since UK Government forbid export of <u>military</u> equipment to Canaan.

Henderson
Managing Director

CONFIDENTIAL

To: Joshua Demolition Co (attention Achan)
From: UK Government – Department of Industrial Enterprise
Date: 2nd Kislev 1241 BC

Have heard on best authority of your wish to purchase goods from Miraculous Tubing. In order to maintain active UK-Canaan trading, suggest future communications stress <u>peaceful</u> nature of your activity.

Best wishes.
Cleric
p.s. Look forward to meeting again at the Armageddon '41 Military Trade Fair.

To: Miraculous Tubing
From: Joshua Peaceful Construction PLC (*please note change in trading title*)
cc: UK Government – Department of Industrial Enterprise
Date: 25th Adar 1241 BC

Purpose of tubing is for urban renewal west of River Jordan. Stress <u>no</u> military function. Need for product now urgent.

Achan

JERICHOGATE

To: Joshua Peaceful Construction PLC
From: Miraculous Tubing, c/o Customs & Excise Remand Centre
cc: UK Government – Department of Industrial Enterprise
Date: 17th Tammuz 1241 BC

Advise delay in delivery due to impounding of tubing by Customs & Excise at docks.

Henderson

To: UK Government – Department of Industrial Enterprise
From: Joshua Peaceful Construction PLC
cc: Miraculous Tubing
Date: 18th Tammuz 1241 BC

Insist on explanation as to seizure of urgently required tubing from UK supplier. Prolonged detainment will necessitate search for alternative manufacturer outside UK.

Achan

CONFIDENTIAL

To: Customs & Excise
From: Department of Industrial Enterprise
Date: 19th Tammuz 1241 BC

Your action re Miraculous Tubing could lead to shut–down of Sheffield plant. UK unemployment already in double figures. Suggest you contemplate <u>all</u> implications for UK Government of your decision and THINK AGAIN!

Cleric

JERICHOGATE

To: Department of Industrial Enterprise
From: Customs & Excise
Date: 30th Tammuz 1241 BC

Thank you for your communication of 19th Tammuz, the contents of which have been noted. The Minister responsible will give the matter urgent consideration when he returns from a fact-finding tour of Sinai in the new year.

p.p. P.P.S. to P.U.S.S., C & E.

To: Miraculous Tubing
From: Joshua Peaceful Construction PLC
cc: Department of Industrial Enterprise
    Customs & Excise
Date: 5th Elul 1241 BC

Cancel order. Belgian supplier located.

Achan

SECRET

To: Customs & Excise
From: Department of Industrial Enterprise
Date: 6th Elul 1241 BC

You bloody w*****s!

Cleric

JERICHOGATE

To: Department of Industrial Enterprise
From: Customs & Excise
Date: 26th Elul 1241 BC

Thank you for your communication of 6th Elul, the contents of which have been noted. The Minister responsible will give the matter urgent consideration when he returns from a fact-finding tour of Sinai in the new year.

p.p. P.P.S. to P.U.S.S., C & E.

To: Miraculous Tubing
From: The Joshua General Engineering Company (*please note change in trading title*)
cc: Department of Industrial Enterprise
    Customs & Excise
Date: 27th Elul 1241 BC

Belgian supplier dead. Please deliver soonest. Have re-confirmed to Customs & Excise tubing required for general engineering work only.

Achan

To: The Joshua General Engineering Company
From: Miraculous Tubing
cc: Department of Industrial Enterprise
    Customs & Excise
Date: 30th Kislev 1241 BC

Tubing released (thanks, we believe, to influence of DIE). Require payment on delivery. Invoice enclosed with product.

Good luck.

Henderson

JERICHOGATE

To: Miraculous Tubing
From: Holy War Enterprises (*please note change in trading title*)
cc: Department of Industrial Enterprise
   Customs & Excise
Date: 1st Shebat 1240 BC

Confirm safe receipt. Payment will follow on completion of project – confident of securing unto our treasury silver and gold and vessels of brass and iron. Have used trumpet daily for past six days. Anticipate multi-use tomorrow to complete venture.

Achan

Can this be the fabled British-designed 'Supertrumpet' that destroyed Jericho?

GARDEN GATE

OR

THE NAZARETH LAZARUS?

The issue of the Crucifixion is a thorny one, such is the risk of causing unintentional offence. Nevertheless we believe we can further advance the many theories put forward in the last few decades about what really *did* happen on that first Good Friday.

The investigations of others have established beyond doubt (at any rate in our own minds) that Jesus was more than just the sheet-and-sandal clad ascetic portrayed in the – highly selective and self-interested – Gospels. It is at least arguable, in the opinion of modern scholars, that he was an aristocrat who married young and was for example having man-to-Son of Man discussions with Pontius Pilate about sending his children away to Rome to be classically educated.

We'd now like to toss our own shekel into the pot: *could it be that Jesus was also a gifted conjuror?*

By this we don't mean that he was a practitioner of the magic arts in any dark satanic sense: that would be absurd. No – we think that Jesus, foreseeing the difficulties involved in this first-ever 'Mission to Explain', decided that the best way would be to sugar the pill: in other words hide the serious messages he was putting across by giving his audience a bit of a laugh and a thrill at the same time.

He could have got the idea at the famous 'Water-into-Wine' wedding, which, as has been persuasively argued elsewhere, was probably that of Jesus himself to Mary Magdalene, a.k.a. Mary of Bethany. In which case the Best Man would have been Mary's brother, one Lazarus.

It is almost certain that Lazarus's speech was a dud: he wouldn't have dared make ribald remarks about the widespread gossip that Mary Magdalene wasn't a virgin (not in front of Jesus's mother Mary, at any rate) and as for the bridegroom, what was there funny to say about him, save a few dry anecdotes about some woodwork that went wrong? (Incidentally, it could well have been the early training in carpentry that gave Jesus his interest in magic, putting false bottoms in drawers and so on: a knack that was to prove invaluable later, at the supposed end of his life.)

The ever-charitable Jesus came to the rescue of his new brother-in-law by diverting the attention of the grumbling guests, apparently changing the water in some stone jars into wine of the finest vintage (the '12). To a magician, this was a simple matter of substitution, though again significant in view of future events. Lazarus must have taken Jesus on one side during the ensuing revels and vowed eternal gratitude, pledging that if there was ever anything he could do in return . . . was this the moment a seed took root in Jesus's mind?

From that time on, his fame spread through the Holy Land and he drew vast crowds wherever he preached. Many of the people brought hopeful pitchers of water, but were well satisfied to be given a free lunch (by now Jesus would have taught his disciples the rudiments of magic and it was easy for twelve men to hide that many loaves and fishes in their raiments). But it was Jesus's 'patter', the parables between the tricks, that would have interested the ruling Romans, realizing that he was concealing dangerous subversion up his sleeve . . .

Jesus must have been aware of the disquiet he was causing amongst the Romans and the dignitaries of Jerusalem – High Priests, wealthy merchants, etc. – whose main interest was to preserve the status quo and not allow the public imagination to be poisoned with nonsense about Do-Gooder Samaritans. This, in our submission, explains Jesus's supposedly strange behaviour when he heard that his brother-in-law Lazarus was ill in Bethany.

What did this celebrated healer of the sick do? He waited two days before paying a house call! In fact, according to St John's Gospel:

> 'On his arrival Jesus found that Lazarus had already been four days in the tomb.'
>
> [11:17]

What's more, Jesus was torn off a strip by his sister-in-law Martha, who said in front of the gathering crowds that if Jesus had arrived earlier her late brother wouldn't now be walled up behind that large rock guarding the tomb's entrance.

As far as we are concerned, Martha might as well have been wearing sequins, so perfectly did she play the role of magician's assistant! Jesus ordered a couple of burly onlookers to – in the words of the Mott the Hoople song – 'Roll Away the Stone'. To quote the Gospel again:

> 'Then he raised his voice in a great cry: "Lazarus, come forth." The dead man came out, *his hands and feet swathed in linen bands, his face wrapped in a cloth.*' [our italics]
>
> [11:43-4]

This might of course have been merely a cheap stunt to amaze the crowd and get them to buy Jesus's good news about the Afterlife. But we think it had much greater significance: that it was nothing less than *a dress rehearsal*.

Within days, Jesus was hauled up before the beak, in the shape of Pontius Pilate, who washed his hands of the case and turned Jesus over to the tender mercies of Caiaphas and Co. But why would he deliberately send to be crucified someone who in all probability had been to dinner *chez* Pilate, might even have performed a few card tricks for the ladies? *Why, unless he was sure Jesus would not be crucified?*

GARDENGATE

We think there is a possibility – we dare put it no stronger – that the Crucifixion was a charade: as the mob swirled round Jesus as he carried the beam of the cross towards the Garden of Gethsemane, he could easily have slipped out of the ropes binding his hands (the beam might even have been specially hinged, a typical magician's prop).

The disguised Lazarus could then have taken Jesus's place, finally repaying his debt for that terrible best man's speech. The distant Garden (a.k.a. 'Green Hill Far Away') would have been the perfect discreet setting for phase two of the plan, as Lazarus hung on the cross for the minimum period before being cut down and put in the tomb – for which his earlier incarceration had prepared him perfectly.

But how do we explain the ringing tones of Jesus on the cross as he looked to heaven and cried: 'It is accomplished!' (John) or 'My God, My God, why hast thou forsaken me?' (Matthew, Mark) or 'Father, into thy hands I commit my spirit' (Luke)?

Easily. The clue is contained in the discrepancy between the Gospels' versions. Jesus would, as a magician (not to mention a gifted storyteller), have been practised in the art of ventriloquism – throwing his voice six feet upwards wouldn't have been a problem. Calling through the disguise of a cloth wrapped round his face was more difficult though, and it is no surprise that the Scribes on the outside of the crowd, recording the scene for posterity, made up the words they couldn't catch.

That night, with Jesus safely out of the country and headed for the Mediterranean, Lazarus would have been released from the tomb, none the worse for wear except a couple of stigmata in his hands and feet (and perhaps not even that – couldn't the 'linen bands' that wrapped his extremities at the dress rehearsal have been hiding the results of acupuncture, to inure him to the pain?).

In fact the only real loser was Judas Iscariot, who had volunteered to add verisimilitude to the scam by 'betraying' Jesus. He then quite properly tried to return his thirty pieces of silver, but made the mistake of adding cockily 'I'm rendering unto Caesar that which is Caesar's.' Smelling a rat, the elders of the temple took him out and hanged him.

Do we have any actual proof that this is how the 'Crucifixion' happened? Not as such. What we do have is a crucial hint in the works of Leonardo da Vinci who, besides all his other distinctions, was also one of the 'Grand Masters of the Prieure of Sion' (cf. *Thatchergate*, p130) and thus privy to this greatest of all secrets. In a sketch for his famous painting *The Last Supper*, Leonardo quite clearly intended to reveal that there were *two* Jesuses (see below).

At first we thought that one of the figures had simply run round the other end, so that he could appear in the picture twice. But this was clearly ridiculous: it was a *painting*. All the food would have gone cold!

The only logical explanation was that among the supper

GARDENGATE

guests was Lazarus, already in full make-up, ready to take his place in the story of the greatest escape of all time. And the other figure at the end of the line-up? It can only have been Jesus's 'body-double', a fail-safe mechanism in case there should be an unforeseen hitch in this most important game of 'Find the Lord'. But Leonardo must have thought better of telling what he knew, lest the devout faith of millions of believers be for ever shattered.

We have no such qualms. In our view this version of the Resurrection only adds to the magnificent mystery of the Life of Our Lord, and makes His determination to cheat even death to keep spreading The Word all the more moving.

There is a well-known American expression: 'Jesus H. Christ'.

DOES THE 'H' STAND FOR 'HOUDINI'?

GRAILGATE

With so many Biblical so-called 'facts' falling by the wayside, thanks to our combination of healthy scepticism and inspired detective work, it seemed an appropriate moment to confront the question that has vexed scholars for nigh on two thousand years.

What DID happen to the Holy Grail?

We think we can provide the answer. We started by disentangling the skeins of supposition about what the Grail actually *was*: one school of thought had it being the cup that Jesus and his disciples drank from at the Last Supper, another that it was the cup used by Joseph of Arimathea to catch the blood of Jesus as he hung on the Cross.

SUPPOSE IT WAS BOTH. . . AND NEITHER?

Before we are accused of blasphemy, let us reiterate our theories about Jesus's escape from death (cf. *Gardengate*, p28). As the evidence suggests, while a decoy was substituted in a way later made famous in the film *Albert, RN*,[1] our Lord could have been smuggled out of Jerusalem. With Him safely out of the way across the water, it fell to the surviving disciples and their converts to preach the message of Christianity to as wide an audience as possible.

One of the most enthusiastic recruits to the cause was St Paul, who in his famous 'Letters' did much to explain what had brought about his own conversion. But we think he did more than that. We think we can reveal exactly why at least one of the Letters – to the Ephesians – had such an impact.

At our request, the science laboratory at one of our most

---

[1] The British film of the 1950s recounting how a soldier escaped from a POW camp, his place taken on the parade ground by a dummy. The special version, which runs five hours, shows all but one of the prisoners escaping, leaving Dickie Attenborough and two hundred and thirty-two dummies.

GRAILGATE

senior universities (which has begged not to be named, for obvious reasons) submitted this Letter, written on papyrus during the first century AD, to all the twenty-first-century, state of the art technology at its disposal. Rarely has the phrase 'reading between the lines' been more appropriate.

This is what became visible under ultra-violet light:

> The Ephesians,
> Ephesia,
> EPH 1AN
>
> Dear EPHESIANS ,
>
> I bring good news! You, the EPHESIANS, have been chosen from all of Christendom to receive this Holy Grail!
>
> Hand-tooled by ancient Phoenician craftsmen, this Grail will grace the EPHESIANS ' home and will be something you will want to pass on to your children and your children's children!
>
> Imagine the envious looks on the faces of the ROMANS , the GALATIANS , and the THESSALONIANS when they see this Holy Grail sitting on the EPHESIANS ' shelf!
>
> Of Surpassing Holiness! The neighbours will beat a path to your door just to touch it!
>
> Recreate the majesty and mystery of the Last Supper in the comfort of your own home!
>
> *Pay no money now!*
>
> The name of the THE EPHESIANS has been

GRAILGATE

entered in a Prize Draw, so you may already have won Eternal Life! And 100 runners-up will each receive one of Our Lord's genuine fingers!

If you feel unable to take up this offer, please pass this Letter on. Do not break the chain, or the Wrath of God will be visited upon THE EPHESIANS in less time than it takes for a camel to pass through the eye of a needle!

Sincerely,

Paul
(formerly trading as Saul) *of Tarsus.*

This clever piece of marketing seems to have had the desired effect, judging by the many thousands of 'converts' who were marching under the banner of Christianity by the turn of the century.

GRAILGATE

And the fact that they *all* had a grail, yet were claiming unique properties and powers for it, would explain the confusion that has arisen during subsequent years – not to mention the fruitlessness of the search for the original by such disparate bodies as the Knights Templar and the self-styled 'Campaign for Real Grail'.

One puzzle remained – how did Paul, who sent out this particular letter from a prison cell, conceal the message in his 'official' words of wisdom? For the answer, we turned to the clue contained in the first few lines.

This may be translated (though, confusingly, it wasn't in the King James New Testament or the New English Bible) as:

> 'Grace to you, and *the peace of the Balm of Gilead*, from God Our Father and the Lord Jesus Christ.'

Intrigued, we went to the Gilead region, east of the River Jordan, and after much haggling managed to obtain a phial of balm – a resinous gum exuded from the original cedars of Lebanon.

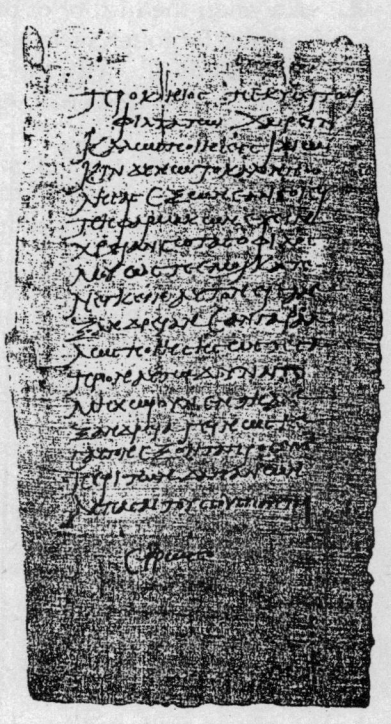

Our audience is probably ahead of us when we confirm that applying a little of the gum to the papyrus Letter does indeed reveal the words of the hidden message, and establishes Paul well and truly as the patron saint of junk mail!

FORESTGATE

Having exploded many of the myths in the Bible, it seemed appropriate that we should turn a sceptical eye on the history of our own country, and see what conveniently forgotten facts we could bring to light. Surely – to start methodically with the As – there must be something significant buried (Sword-in-Stone like) in the Arthurian legend?

Alas no – apart from a scurrilous and crudely-written rumour we found stitched to the inside of a faded piece of animal skin, wrapped round an ale firkin in the Glastonbury Folk Museum. The work of one 'Regan', it alleged that King Arthur was so under the thumb of Queen Guinevere that he let her determine Round Table policy, after following the astrological advice of her personal magician Merlin.

Such an idea was clearly fantastical if not actually deranged, and we set off in frustration on the long journey back to London. Our mood was not improved by a strange phenomenon: whichever way we turned, the road seemed to draw us back towards Wiltshire – and specifically, in the direction of Stonehenge.

The power of ley-lines harnessed to the phase of the moon – or merely an incompetent navigator? It seemed to be the latter, until the fifth or sixth wrong turning brought us out in the Dorset village of Cerne Abbas.

It also brought us to nothing less than an apprehension of the possible origins of our Island Race.

FORESTGATE

The road runs alongside the enormous chalk carving of the Cerne Giant, and the appearance of this virile figure set us thinking: was there some message for us? Was he a sentinel perhaps, or a signpost pointing back to some as yet undiscovered facet of history?

The answer was not long in coming. It was now getting dark, and the hilly fields around the Giant were completely deserted. As we pondered, a man suddenly appeared on the right foot of the Giant. He was pushing in front of him one of those wheeled contraptions still used on some roads for repainting the white lines. While we watched, he proceeded to 'touch up' every inch of the Giant, leaving it gleaming as new. The obvious question occurred: just how ancient was this man-made artefact? Was he really the result of vandalism by Dark Age Travellers?

When the workman had gone, we clambered up the hillside and took a sample of the chalk from underneath the fresh paint. A friendly police forensic department later confirmed our suspicions: the so-called 'chalk' was actually a type of blanco, *the substance used by the military that wasn't even in existence before the twentieth century*!

Fired by the thought of yet another cover-up, we scoured newspaper libraries for anything that might explain why it was necessary to 'invent' this Giant – had there been another one, for instance, which might throw a less than flattering light on our antecedents?

Indeed there had. In a late 1960s issue of the *Walthamstow*

FORESTGATE

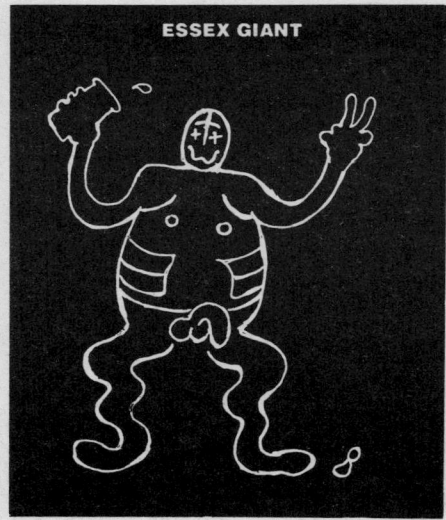

Gazette we found a strange story about some motorcycle scramblers who had stumbled across the outline of a huge human head, after one of their number had ploughed his bike in to the side of a hill in Epping Forest. It was strange because the next day there was a follow-up story about excited archaeologists descending on the site and excavating more of the figure . . .

Then complete silence.

Clearly, there was something about this 'Essex Giant' that had to be suppressed. We went to the Headquarters of the Archaeological Association and sat in the reception area until finally they agreed to show us their files from that particular date. Sure enough, there was the record of what could only be described as a major discovery.

And yet, within weeks, plans for a new motorway, the M11, were swiftly pushed through and this area of great natural beauty (not to mention historical significance) was buried under concrete.

Why? Was there something shameful in the possibility that we might all be descended from Essex Man? Would Winston Churchill's seminal work have to be retitled *A History of the Estuary-English Speaking Peoples*? We could only surmise – but our appetite had been whetted and as the reader will discover, more Giants with startling tales to tell lay just below the surface of this green and pleasant land . . .

ARROWGATE

It has always seemed odd to many people that umbrellas are banned from art galleries. (What damage could one do to a picture with an umbrella which one could not do with, say, a four-foot-long aluminium crutch?) What we have discovered is that this universal brolly-ban apparently originated at the Victoria and Albert Museum, South Kensington. And in learning this nugget of information, we also became privy to the facts behind yet another conspiracy of immense proportion.

In 1842 the Bayeux Tapestry was exhibited for the first time properly at the Hotel de Ville in Bayeux. A curator from the Victoria and Albert Museum was sent over to inspect the historic embroidery and to take a full set of photographs for the British Government. Being prepared for any kind of nasty foreign weather, the curator had with him his umbrella with which he idly unwound the tapestry, looking for the good bits. Suddenly, the tip of the umbrella caught in the ancient material and, before long, yards of coloured twine were draped across the floor. Bending down to inspect the damage (and vowing never to allow umbrellas in *his* museum again) the curator was amazed to find a whole new layer of tapestry beneath the tangled surface, telling a whole new story of the Battle of Hastings. Photographs were taken of this, the *true* Bayeux Tapestry, and sent back in complete secrecy to the V & A. It was to be another twenty-nine years before the 'damage' was repaired and official snaps taken of the reconstructed version, from which all reproductions have since been made.

ARROWGATE

We are grateful to the gentlemen in the cloakroom of the Victoria and Albert Museum who – on seeing the umbrellas we ourselves were attempting to take into the Throne Room Exhibition last year – took us to one side, told us the above story, and provided us with photocopies of the original Bayeux Tapestry photographs which now allow us to reveal what *really* happened at Hastings. In other words, who shot KH?

An outstanding soldier, sound administrator and brave warrior, King Harold was hallowed by his contemporaries, who may have seen in his accession to the throne the creation of a new Camelot. But it was a dream that was to be cruelly shattered one chilly afternoon in September 1066, when a lone archer supposedly penetrated the watertight security cordon surrounding the King, and ended the hopes of a generation.

But what exactly happened that afternoon in Hastings? No one could remember precisely what they were doing when the King of England was assassinated; the news took nearly two decades to reach some peasant settlements in Rutland.

But still questions continued to nag the eleventh-century man-in-the-dirt-track: 'How could it happen?' 'Why did it happen?' 'Where's England?' Luckily for us, the *real* Bayeux Tapestry provides a snapshot of events leading up to the death of KH. Through detailed frame-by-frame analysis we can piece together the truth behind one of the greatest cover-ups since Cnut nearly drowned.

The 'facts' are well known. The authorities would have us believe that King Harold was killed by a single arrow in the eye, fired by a lone marksman operating from a distance some 80 metres away (Frames 1 & 2). But the moment of death (Frame 1) is revealing. On closer inspection we can see four arrows hitting King Harold: although the fatal blow is certainly to the eye, one cannot avoid the conclusion that there were others who were determined to kill the King. Ballistics experts support this theory, confirming it would be impossible for a single archer to fire off four arrows simultaneously.

ARROWGATE

FRAME 1: The Four Arrows

FRAME 2: The Lone Archer

ARROWGATE

FRAME 3: The 'Magic Arrow'

Other doubts surround the fatal arrow itself. For an archer firing at ground level, the missile would have to follow an extraordinary trajectory in order to hit Harold at eye level (Frame 3). It would, indeed, have to be a 'magic arrow'. Far more likely is the theory that a group of archers, operating from a much closer vantage point, had a clear view of the King and his highly-trained Saxon Security Advisers (SSA). Working together, they could fire off round after round of volleys, while the SSA men were distracted by a Norman cavalry charge. And where better to shoot the King than from behind the trees on the grassy knoll (Frame 4)? Who is the suspicious figure lurking on the knoll? How do we know that there are not more accomplices hidden directly behind the tree itself? And why is the Bayeux Tapestry – so illuminating on details such as the arrival of Halley's Comet – so silent on this matter?

Other unanswered questions remain. Shortly before the volley of arrows hits King Harold, a man is seen to duck mysteriously – as if he were forewarned of events to come (Frame 5). Was he, too, an accomplice in the assassination? And what of the man with the umbrella in Frame 6? By all accounts it was a sunny day. Was he giving some sort of signal

ARROWGATE

Frame 4: The Grassy Knoll

ARROWGATE

FRAMES 5 and 6: The Ducking Man and
The Man with the Umbrella

to the marksmen perched hidden from view on the grassy knoll?

One explanation alone provides the answers: that KH was killed by a conspiracy led by the Norman pre-industrial military complex. War in the Middle Ages was big business. From the tapestry itself we can see the enormous energy involved in boat-building and re-armament. Yet Harold didn't want war. When he succeeded to the throne, he did so in the hope that nobody would mind very much. He would rather not have had a fight. So, faced with the crippling of the Norman war machine in an indefinite peace, big business had no option but to dispatch men to Hastings to terminate the peacemonger.

Far-fetched? Perhaps. But perhaps not. One chilling fact suggests a more sinister rationale of events. All the witnesses to the incidents on that September afternoon in 1066 have, without exception, conveniently died. A coincidence? Or is it another one in the eye for those who would know the truth?

POKERGATE

The sad – nay, tragic – story of King Edward II has often been told, with his horrific demise featuring blood, gore and hot metal. But the real tragedy lies in the fact that Edward's death was not the result of a murderous plot, nor indeed any kind of conspiracy. It was simply a lamentable accident.

The truth has only recently come to light following the discovery of a libretto and set designs for a musical written by Guillaume de Machaut in 1329. The brilliant composer de Machaut was a priest who originated the polyphonic mass and was responsible for some of the best-loved works of musical theatre in the fourteenth century, including *Jesu Christe – Rextremendaemajestatis* and *Madonna* (cf. *Brandenburg-Gate*, p73).

In 1306 Edward decided not to complete his training course for the Knights Templar and (together with close personal friend Gascon Piers Gaveston) resigned his commission. His father, Edward I, was furious and tore out handfuls of his son's hair, giving him a distinctive bald patch which was to cause much of the ridicule he suffered in later years.

The younger Edward searched in vain for a worthwhile occupation and eventually became apprenticed to de Machaut as an assistant stage manager at Rheims cathedral (commuting from the home he shared with his parents in central London). He quickly learnt how to make a good cup of tea, but little else.

Responding to cruel suggestions of an unhealthy relationship with Gaveston, Edward took a wife – Isabella – in 1308, hoping that such a move would scotch the vicious rumours. It did not, and allegations of homosexuality pursued him to his grave.

POKERGATE

Taking the throne in 1307, King Edward II (as he then became) was forced to put his theatrical ambitions on the back burner and concentrate on running England. Sadly, he was ill equipped for such an onerous responsibility and the country quickly went to the dogs.

His friend Gaveston was executed in 1311 and the other Queen in his life, Isabella, was far from supportive. At the Battle of Bannockburn in 1314 his army was humiliated by the Scots, thanks to the participation on the Scottish side of French and English Knights Templar. Edward appealed against the result, claiming the opposition had fielded too many foreign players, but the referee's decision was upheld.

Over the next thirteen years public opinion swung further and further against Edward until he found himself forced to make one last desperate bid to regain a modicum of popularity.

He decided to organize a festival of games in which the entire Royal family and their favourites would participate, thus showing them all to be 'ones of the people'.

Guerres Sans Frontières
Jousting with the red-hot lance.
Did Edward turn tail?

POKERGATE

Shooting the apple blindfold

Walking the greasy pole over the pit of red-hot pokers. Can this be how Edward met his end?

The teams for these 'Guerres Sans Frontières' (as they were called in an attempt to attract a French audience) were captained by Queen Isabella, her close personal friend Roger Mortimer, Hugh Despenser the younger, and Edward himself.

POKERGATE

The set designs for the de Machaut musical about the last years of the King (*Edward and His Amazing Bloodspattered Armour*) reveal the extraordinarily dangerous games that were dreamt up for the festival, and it is hardly surprising that there were so many fatalities – Robert Lewer was crushed to death beneath heavy stones; Hugh Despenser was castrated; the Earl of Pembroke died suddenly whilst sitting on a privy; and Edward, of course, slipped whilst tackling the 'Hot Poker Run'.

INTERESTING FOOTNOTE

In one of those strange quirks of fate that we have (almost) grown accustomed to in the course of writing this book, another mystery has been cleared up by the de Machaut musical.

In the heart-rending final scene, the freshly widowed Queen Isabella faces up to the task of making ends meet without a King to support her. She decides to run a laundry for noblemen and takes in her first batch of washing just a week after Edward's death. Having washed a sheet, she looks for a hard surface on which to iron it (ironing boards not yet having been invented). Close at hand is the stiff corpse of her late husband and she rests the sheet on that whilst applying the hot iron. To her dismay, an imprint of Edward appears through the thin material and she is forced to refund the owner and throw away the sheet.

Put that piece of evidence with the fact that the so-called Turin Shroud has been shown by carbon-dating to originate from the fourteenth century and one more puzzle bites the dust: the image on the shroud is Edward II.

POKERGATE

Just in case anyone requires further proof, this computer-enhanced image of the Shroud shows quite clearly the face of a man who not only fits the description of King Edward II but also appears to have been surprised by something unpleasant at the moment of his death.

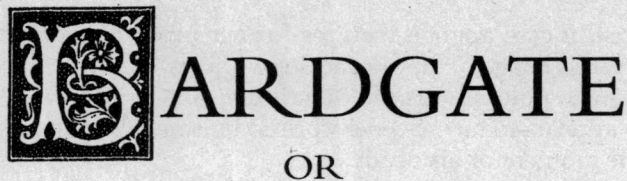ARDGATE
OR
'Fie, Honey, I'm Home!'

Exhausted by the sheer number of lids we were now obliged to lift, we thought we deserved a break and took ourselves off to the local cinema for the afternoon. It was a special schools matinée screening of Kenneth Branagh's *Much Ado About Nothing*, and amid all the scenes of roistering and sexual shenanigans one boy (who was watching the film instead) asked his teacher the 64,000 ducat question:

> 'Why aren't Shakespeare's comedies *funny*?'

We think we can supply the answer.

Close examination of the original quarto manuscripts of his play *Henry V*, and further comparison with the 'official' Folio printed text, brought to light some fascinating and major discrepancies: nothing less than a major sub-plot involving the wives of the 'comic relief' characters Nym, Pistol and Bardolph.

The conventional wisdom is that Shakespeare dropped these scenes for reasons of length after the first performance – which went on beyond midnight, and the 'groundlings' in the Globe Theatre grumbled that they had missed their last walk home. Certainly there is evidence that Shakespeare intended to reshape the material into a separate comedy, working title *The Merry Wives of Chigwell*.

So why didn't he? First let us study a segment of the text:

ACT I

SCENE I

Chigwell. A kitchen. SHARON PISTOL sits at a table, biting the heads off turnips from a basket and dropping the rest on the floor.

Enter TRACY NYM.

TRACY: Sir Gordon Bennett, Shar! Why must every chamber you tether your great bottom in befind itself more noisome than a jakes?

[*Mirth*]

SHARON: Leave 't out, Trace. I'm in an ill humour.
TRACY: Go to, go to. Unless I'm much mistook, the apple of thine eye may even now be pierced by a French lance. Or Wayne, come to think on't.

[*Mirth*]

SHARON: You ever been to Agincourt, Trace?
TRACY: No nearer than a sack of mead brought back on St Vitus' Day, sans a ha'porth of duty paid.

[*Mirth*]

Flourish: Enter DORIEN BARDOLPH.

SHARON: How now, what, art come already, Ancient Dorien?
DORIEN: Ancient I am not, I thank you, except when Zephyr's cheeks blow in the wrong direction. And as for coming, my portals are as Master Sainsbury's bread shelf Saturday twelve-noon.

[*Mighty mirth*]

TRACY: Do what, pardee?
SHARON: She means empty.

BARDGATE

DORIEN: Ay, emptier than a plucked teazle that has sat too long i' the woodchucky thicket. Handy-dandy! But how will I ever find a forked creature with all bod cons? Come on, girls, smite your pates and bethink yourselves trouserwards.

TRACY: Marry, I will.

SHARON: I would as lief not again, if I had the chance. I said I would as lief not *marry* again, if I had the chance.

[*Slight mirth*]

TRACY: Rabbit rabbit.

DORIEN: I would fain reproduce so fast!

[*Mighty mirth*]

TRACY: Let us be daughters of the adage: 'When the cat away is, the mice play will'. Do we believe that our husbands will be personating the popinjay mewed up outside Chastity's Gate? And on the eve of battle? Fadge! Let's go a-clicking!

DORIEN: Already my loins froth and curdle like the oil of the Persian But Tracy, all the swains left behind in Albion are long i' th' tooth, or bandy-legged, or look like Captain Brinkum-Brankum after a poisoned gaudy!

[*Mighty mirth*]

TRACY: I have a schemato that every knave in Chigwell's bailiwick will run to when he hears!

DORIEN: Surmisest thou the same as me?

TRACY: I' faith, I do.

SHARON: Well let me in on it, you brace of Hecate's afterbirths!

TRACY: What do we think, Dor'? She can be a thrice-staled blanket, high days and holidays alike.

DORIEN: Oh, tell her. Else peace will be like pork at Passover.

TRACY: An Earthenware party!!

[*Mirth, thunderflashes and excursions*]

BARDGATE

It seems bizarre that this crisply written comedy, with its jokes all smoothly engineered and functioning perfectly, should never have seen the light of day. And that the self-styled Swan of Avon should have preferred to inflict on the public limp entertainments like *Twelfth Night* and *Much Ado*. Unless – and this is where we are convinced we have made a major breakthrough in Shakespearean studies – unless:

THE MERRY WIVES OF CHIGWELL WAS THE WORK OF ANOTHER HAND.

After considerable research, we have concluded that Shakespeare's 'ghost' and, let's face it, comic peer, was not as might be expected Francis Bacon, or Beaumont and Fletcher, or Ben Jonson, but an unsung and indeed *unnamed* writer, seen here in a contemporary artist's impression:

BARDGATE

In other words, there was more than a grain of truth in the old saying 'Give fifty thousand monkeys fifty thousand pens for fifty thousand years and one of them will eventually write *Macbeth*'. It is our submission that one of them could have done – or at any rate was the comic genius behind the *funny Merry Wives*.

Monkeys were well known for being talented creatures in the seventeenth century (cf. *Aldgate*, p62) and it would clearly have been professional jealousy that caused Shakespeare to sever the partnership and suppress the manuscript, finding the concept of *Bards of a Feather* demeaning.

And the monkey? It is highly probable that he passed on all his expertise to his descendants – *some of whom may even be writing comedy today* . . .

In the mean time, let us propose an addition to the dictionary of quotations: 'Shakespeare without the monkey is like *Hamlet* without the Prince of Denmark'!

TRAITOR'S GATE
THE TRUE STORY OF THE GUNPOWDER PLOT PLOT

We were sitting in the Public Gallery of the House of Lords one afternoon, hoping to ambush a reclusive peer of the realm who had so far managed to avoid helping us with our enquiries (alas we never did track him down, and Archergate must remain a closed chapter until a future volume). Suddenly we were awoken by a loud knocking on an outer door. A small squabble over who should go and open it proved unnecessary, as the door was thrown wide to reveal a figure clad in knee-britches carrying a long wand topped with a gold lion. Black Rod, of course. And this apparition set us thinking about the Mother of all Parliaments, its traditions and how easily it could have become a blackened, redundant ruin, almost four centuries ago . . .

TRAITOR'S GATE

At first sight the case of Guy Fawkes could not be more open and shut. Explosives were planted in a cellar beneath the House of Lords, set with a slow fuse that would give Fawkes and his fellow-conspirators time to escape, foregather at Tamworth and then march on a government-less London at the head of a band of rebels. They would then seize the reins of power and put a Roman Catholic monarch on the throne.

However, tipped off by a mysterious letter, Lord Salisbury the Prime Minister ordered the cellar to be searched. Fawkes was discovered, the matches on him ready to light the fuse. Taken to the Tower of London and tortured, Fawkes revealed the names of his treacherous colleagues: Robert Catesby, Thomas Percy, John and Christopher Wright, Robert and Thomas Winter, Ambrose Rookwood and Robert Keyes. The conspirators hid in a house in Stourbridge, but were flushed out by the Sheriff of Warwickshire and his men and died in a hail of musket bullets. Those who escaped were later executed. Fawkes himself was hanged, drawn and quartered.

Such were the facts. Or so it seemed until a copy of Government papers fell into our hands, from out of a bush by the side of a canal towpath. They had hitherto been kept from the public under the 'Five Hundred Year Rule'. They give a very different view of the Gunpowder Plot, and the supposed guilt of what will inevitably become known as 'The Westminster Nine'.

To start with Fawkes himself. When taken to the Tower, he insisted that he had merely been a caretaker at the House of Lords and had been locking up when arrested. Traces of gunpowder beneath his fingernails gave the lie to this story. However, it is our strong belief that this evidence was only discovered after torture, in other words THE GUNPOWDER WAS PLANTED ON HIS FINGERNAILS WHEN THEY HAD BEEN REMOVED!

TRAITOR'S GATE

And consider the evidence of Fawkes's so-called 'confession':

SERJEANT-AT-ARMS: If your purpose was an innocent one, chummy, why did you carry on your person the means to make fire?

FAWKES: I had obtained it at the apothecary's shop, after being invited to a friend's house to try out a new experience.

CONSTABLE-AT-ARMS: And the name of this friend?

FAWKES: Walter Raleigh.

SERJEANT-AT-ARMS: Never heard of him.

CONSTABLE-AT-ARMS: Import/Export, Sarge. Do anything to get a knighthood.

SERJEANT-AT-ARMS: A likely story, sunshine. Show him the rack, Constable.

FAWKES: OKAY I ADMIT IT, I DONE IT! IT'S A FAIR BEEFEATER! I DONE THE PRINCES-IN-THE-TOWER BLAG AN' ALL! THEY WAS ASKING FOR IT, LITTLE BLEEDERS! YOU GOT ME BANG TO RIGHTS!

SERJEANT-AT-ARMS: Don't you mean 'right to bangs'?

CONSTABLE-AT-ARMS: Nice one, Sarge.

It will be seen at once that this confession was crudely doctored at a later date. Once we had established the bogusness of the police evidence, the rest of the case against Fawkes started to fall apart.

Take for example the 'getaway vehicle'. History records that having planted the device and lit the fuse, Fawkes was to travel post-haste to the Midlands and the rebel army. Yet parked outside the Houses of Parliament was this strange contraption:

TRAITOR'S GATE

Vehicle illegally parked on double brown lines.
Vehicle taken into custody on suspicion of pram-raiding.

Hardly the mode of transport a criminal mastermind would have chosen!

The more thought we devoted to this, the more clear it became that the plot was actually directed *against* the conspirators. Fawkes, Catesby and company were already well-known Roman Catholic sympathizers – what easier way to whip up Protestant support than for the Government to accuse the RCs of instigating a bombing campaign on the mainland? Fawkes was charged under his Spanish-derived name of 'Guido', but in some news-sheets of the time it was deliberately misprinted as 'Guid O'Fawkes'.

As for the alleged letter (or coded message) of warning that was passed on to Lord Salisbury, we have good reason to believe that he himself wrote it, and had it forwarded back to his office by an intermediary. The letter conveniently gave the time and the place of the explosion – 5th November 1605 – but here Salisbury was too clever. The law officers misinterpreted '1605' as 'five past four' and pounced on an empty cellar! Desperate measures were needed to find a culprit.

And this brings us to the most extraordinary revelation of all:

> THERE IS NO REAL PROOF
> THAT GUY FAWKES EXISTED.

Confession, fingernails – all could well have been invented, in the interests of creating a bogeyman whose name would reverberate through the centuries as a warning against the alternatives to Parliamentary democracy. A government campaign of deliberate misinformation, in other words.

What leads us to this conclusion? This remarkable group portrait of the Gunpowder Plotters, setting the mythical Fawkes among the other (well-documented) traitors:

Guy Fawkes – the Original Man in the Stocking Mask!

Aldgate

The Diary of Samuel Pepys is an interesting – if over-long – record of the seventeenth century. What was thought to be the complete manuscript of the Diary is kept at Magdalene College, Cambridge. Of greater importance, however, are the *missing extracts*.

In July 1660, Pepys moved into official lodgings in the Navy Office building (he was a civil servant in that department). These were located in Seething Lane in the City of London. For nearly three centuries, the rooms occupied by Pepys were preserved as they had been at his death. But in 1939, war was declared and it was decided to move all Pepys's furniture to a safe place. A tube station was thought the best storage location to offer protection from the Blitz, the nearest one being Aldgate. The station staff were only too happy to furnish their rest room with seventeenth-century tallboys and, to make more room for their powdered eggs and Woolton Pie ingredients, they emptied the drawers. Finding at the base of each drawer pages of paper with scrawled short-hand on them, they filed them with the weekly season ticket applications . . . and promptly forgot all about them (along with the weekly season ticket applications). These pages were, in fact, yet more entries for Pepys's diary which his foolish servant, Jane Birch, had mistaken for discarded shopping lists.

For the first time, we can reveal a description of events in the 1660s which sheds new light on old disasters. We are grateful to London Transport for allowing us access to their files and recommend that any interested historian hurry along to Aldgate Tube Station and ask, as we did, to look at the 'Ps' in the Zones 1 & 2 pending pile.

ALDGATE

This day, I did see yet more red crosses upon the doors of my neighbours. The plague has come to the city and the cause of this dread sickness is oft discussed. Much thought is that one number from the waytes[1] of Brighton was the carrier of the plague to London. It is rumoured that he did have an unnatural friendship with the monkee he allowed to dance and perform upon his harpsicon, encouraging the beast to play upon both his instrumentes. The crowds who gathered to enjoy the musique, and to watch the fancy pirouettes of the small creature, knew naught of the revolting activitee which occurred between man and beast whenever the wayte became foxed.[2] Apparently, but six months afore I write this, the poor fellow found himself with the clap[3] (as he then thought) and to London brought it, leaving the monkee to its own dread devices by the sea. A doctor here pronounced him ill, but not with the clap. Nor could the good Doctor find a definition for this pestilent ague,[4] minding only to call it 'plague'. Whereupon the ill-mannered (and ill-bodied) wretch set off his rest to share the disease with all the prostitutes of London, finding the city too short in number of monkees I presume. Now, there is scarce an household in the vicinitee which does not carry the red cross to indicate that the plague is within.

[8 November 1665]

The wayte is dead. Every noise of musique[5] in England is for London bound where they intend to honour his memoree with a concert of immense proportion. The good people of the city are to be asked to pay a much-inflated fee for entrance whereupon the funds accumulated will pay for medicine to provide reliefe, and counteract the plague (which took some seven thousand poor souls to their graves this past month).

[14 July 1666]

1. Town musicians   2. Drunk   3. Gonorrhoea
4. Fever   5. Band of performers

ALDGATE

To the Theatre for 'Musique Reliefe', as it was at first descripted upon the wall bills. But within the month, some brighte fool did rename the event 'Red Groin Day' and we are all bidden to paint our yards[6] crimson, which to my mind does scarce honour those who were stroke sick. Yet Drury Lane was packed fit to burst with insipid dolts who had succumbed to the request and who flaunted their tinted members without shame. I chose merely to wear upon my trouser a ribbon of scarlet which is, I think, more becoming to a public servant.

The crowd outside the Theatre rendered entrance impossible and there was much embittered shouting at the men who staffed the doors and gates. The cause of this disquiet was the price for admission – 30 shillings. And for what? Pelham Humfrey hath refused to play. And the so-named 'Souper-Consorte' was nought but Messrs Jagge, Johne and Bowee giving a snapp of musique on virginalls and lute.

The ill-tempered Irishman, Gedforl, did appear at the stage door to shout: 'People are dying. Give us your foxing money. Now.' At this the crowd revolted and their roll tobacco (which everyone does smoke to ward off the plague) was hurled with great vigour at Gedforl. I fear the Theatre did take light for I could smell a pungent odour as I left the ugly scene.

[1 September 1666]

---

6. Penises

ALDGATE

Fieeuw – what a scorcher. And yet, despite the dread condition of the flaming city, my servant Bell felt inclined to decorate upon the wall of his room a lighthearted illustration. I did give Bell a sound lesson about his forbearing to give due solemnitee at such a horrid time.

[4 September 1666]

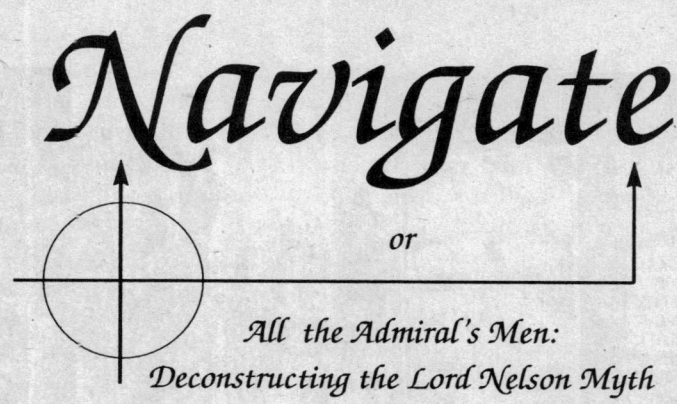

Navigate

or

All the Admiral's Men:
Deconstructing the Lord Nelson Myth

Take a trip to Portsmouth and you'll find the HMS *Victory* Theme Park and Wonderworld, where divorcees and their children queue for hours to share the 'Nelson Experience' – the sounds and smells of battle and life below decks, all lovingly recreated.

While the offspring of our former marriages played happily on the quarterdeck, we resolved to go – literally – behind the scenes, remembering school trips to Pompeii where only the teachers were vouchsafed a look at the more salacious mosaics.

Sure enough, the curator of the Experience confessed that there were documents – fragments of diaries, log-books, suppressed despatches – that added up to a much more three-dimensional picture (to put it at its politest) of one of England's greatest heroes. After making certain arrangements, we were allowed into a secret compartment just aft of the captain's cabin, on a solemn undertaking that we wouldn't note down any of the things we saw there.

We therefore employed the ultra-painstaking attention-to-detail methods of our heroes, Carl Woodward and Bob Bernstein, pooling recollected information after one of their famous off-the-record interviews – and, like them, we think there is an important story to be told here, for which the world has waited too long.

NAVIGATE

One of the main sources of new information was the personal diary of a young lieutenant named Punting who served in every one of Nelson's ships after he took command of HMS *Badger* in 1778. According to Punting's disillusioned final entry, Nelson was nothing less than 'a jackanapes of all the perversions' – though, as we shall see, this judgment may well be coloured by a touch of jealousy towards a particular fellow-officer.

However, Punting's startling main assertion is that *Nelson never missed an opportunity to have a limb sliced off*! We all know that he lost his right eye at Corsica when commanding HMS *Agamemnon* – what nobody knew till now is that he only had a bit of grit in it in the first place. The ship's doctor had suggested getting it out with a damp rag but Nelson demanded the socket be cleared completely.[1]

A few years later at Santa Cruz de Tenerife in the Canary Islands a bullet grazed Nelson's right elbow. He immediately called for a midshipman to chop off the whole arm with his cutlass. When the man hesitated, Nelson grabbed the cutlass with his left hand and an oath, and did the job himself – and according to Punting seemed to quite enjoy the experience. Even his loyal second-in-command and dining companion Captain Hardy felt things were getting too much when, at the Battle of the Nile, Nelson suffered a glancing blow to the forehead and called out: 'Decapitate me, Hardy.'

Punting does concede that Nelson put his 'different abilities' to good use: there was the incident at Copenhagen when the order came through via a 'Fleet Attack Command Signal' (or FACS) to cease hostilities. When a messenger attempted to hand it to him Nelson dangled his empty right sleeve in front of the man's nose and said, 'I have only one arm – I am armless.' The men became hysterical at this joke and, buoyed up by laughter, continued to attack with renewed vigour.

---

[1] The doctor's name was Robert Jay – could he have been the inventor of the multipurpose cloth?

Nelson returned to England in triumph, was immediately made a viscount and – according to a late eighteenth-century listings pamphlet of whose existence we had previously been unaware – did two weeks of stand-up comedy at 'Les Jongleurs' coffee house off-off-Whitehall. His self-mocking one-armed, one-eyed jokes went down a storm with Whig audiences who, due to the unfortunate maladies surrounding King George III, had become afraid to laugh at any form of disability

A contemporary advertisement

For this he won the 'Spa Water' Award inaugurated by the *Observer* newspaper, but the Admiralty was not amused, forbade him to accept the award and ordered him to stand by in Naples. By this time Nelson had fallen under the spell of

Lady Emma Hamilton, who accompanied him to Italy in the guise of a freelance tithe consultant. For this information we are indebted to a now completely forgotten contemporary scandal-sheet called *The Moon*, a few pages of which are also preserved in the secret collection.

The Moon sent a reporter-cum-water colourist in pursuit of the couple, and he struck gold when he found Emma relaxing in Horatio's arm beside a rock pool. As we remember it, he filed the following sensational copy:

The public was shocked, and not even a rescue operation – in which the loyal Captain Hardy took a journalist from *Good Morrow!* magazine round the luxuriantly furnished mews house he shared with Nelson in Little Venice – could repair the damage. Nelson's reputation was ruined and the house stoned by a mob (this gave rise, incidentally, to the so-called 'Curse of *Good Morrow*'). Nelson simply had to get back to sea and try and lose another extremity.

Fortunately a wind called Napoleon Bonaparte was blowing around the Strait of Gibraltar.

From what we can gather from Punting's diaries – bearing in mind his barely concealed resentment at being left out of the Nelson/Hardy decision-making process – much of the donkey work in tracking Napoleon's fleet had been done by the British Task Force under Admiral 'Randy' Collingwood by the time Nelson arrived to take charge at Cadiz. But Nelson soon had the tactical brainwave which was to ensure his everlasting notoriety.

He established an 'Exclusion Zone' and informed the French Commander, Admiral Villeneuve, by carrier pigeon – which was later sautéed in a little red wine and herbs and enjoyed by senior officers on board Villeneuve's ship, the *General Bucentaure*. What they didn't realise was that their goose was cooked as well: Nelson's idea was that the Zone extended in a 200-yard radius not round Gibraltar but round HMS *Victory* – it was a *mobile* Exclusion Zone which Nelson could move at will!

Thus on 21st October 1805, when Villeneuve led the French and Spanish ships north away from Gibraltar – safely outside the Zone as far as he was concerned – Nelson steered the *Victory* to Cape Trafalgar and lay in wait.

When the *General Bucentaure* was within 199 yards of the *Victory*, Nelson ordered his men to open fire, after sending the famous signal 'England Expects That Every Man Will Do His Duty'.

According to Punting this had a coded acronymic meaning for his companion following behind, and Nelson was secretly saying 'Enemy Engaged – Take Extreme Measures. When Destroyed Hardy . . . Dinner?' though this seems to us a little *too* paranoid.

NAVIGATE

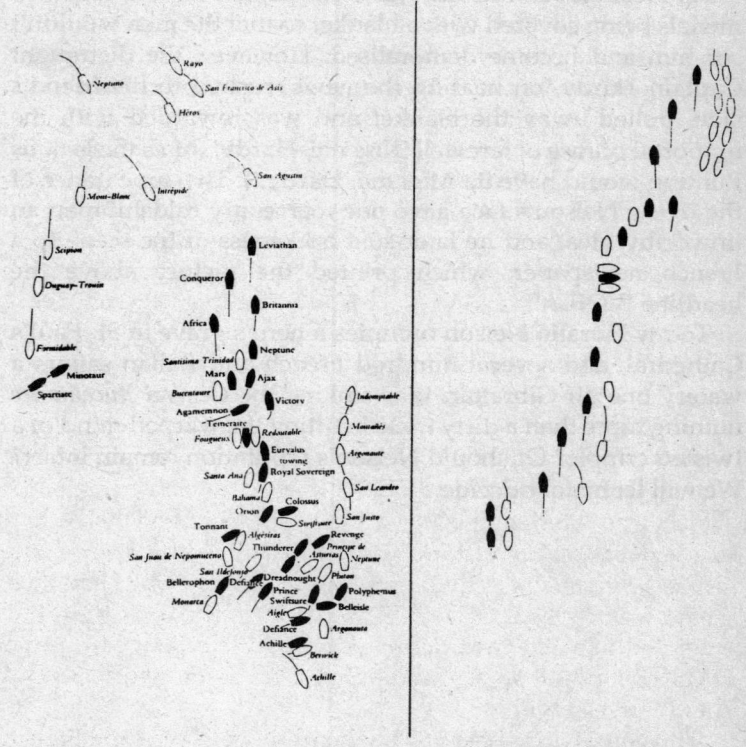

The Trafalgar battle-plan: Nelson makes a ballet out of a crisis

Whatever the truth of the matter, this was one engagement that Nelson didn't keep – the commander of the French ship *Redoubtable*, realizing Nelson's game, took care to stay 201 yards away from the *Victory* and brought out a prototype long-range musket. This had the additional advantage of being able to fire seven rounds instead of six and thus confuse the enemy. The 'Six-ou-Sept' worked perfectly: seeing the first half-dozen shots whistle past harmlessly, Nelson turned his back, and was mortally wounded.

NAVIGATE

As Nelson was carried below he insisted on his face and medals being covered with a blanket so that the men wouldn't see him and become demoralised. However, the distraught Captain Hardy, on hearing the news, rushed to his friend's side, pulled away the blanket and was rewarded with the immortal phrase of farewell 'Kiss me, Hardy' (or as the jealous Punting would have it, '*Miss* me, Hardy.'). The appearance of the dying Nelson's face gave one mercenary midshipman an unworthy idea, and he later sold a likeness of the scene to a French newspaper, which printed the picture above the headline 'VOILA!'

Today Horatio Nelson occupies a hero's grave in St. Paul's Cathedral, and several hundred French and Italian sailors a watery one off Gibraltar. Was sinking the *General Bucentaure* nothing more than a dirty trick, befitting the warped mind of a twisted cripple? Or should Nelson's reputation remain intact? We will let history decide.

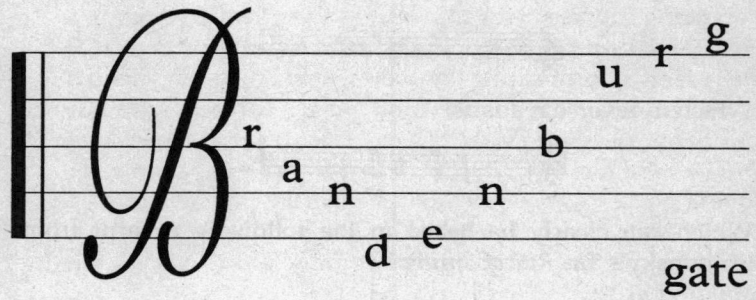

Brandenburg gate

In a moment of relaxation between chapters, we were listening to a recording of Stravinsky's *The Rite of Spring*, thinking (quite foolishly) that the world of classical music was a conspiracy-free zone and might offer us a brief respite from our toils.

And then, we heard it!

A passage from the Introduction (just before figure 12 for those of you who can read music) sounded strangely familiar. Playing it over and over again we could hear five notes which were – without question – the same five notes familiar to us from a modern-day musical currently being performed in London's West End . . . *but in reverse order*!

What had we stumbled on? Quickly, dozens of musical scores were studied and, sure enough, the same notes from the Stravinsky were in works by composers such as Mozart, Beethoven, Bach, Debussy and Manilow. It was as if a code was being passed down a line from age to age, composer to composer. But why? Could it be that there was some secret order to which composers belonged and this code of musical notes was the signal with which they greeted each other? It was quite possible.

BRANENDURG-GATE

Theme from the West End Musical:

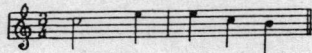

Which in reverse reads as:

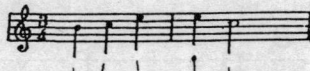

Which can clearly be heard in the following excerpt from Stravinsky's *The Rite of Spring*:

BRANDENBURG-GATE

But – and this was the interesting point – not *every* composer used the notes found in The Rite of Spring. Gustav Holst, Sibelius, Mantovani and Bruckner all chose *not* to include the phrase shown above. Why?

The answer was clear. All composers may join the secret order of musical creators but only the best – the 'Grand Masters' – may pass on and use the secret codes of musical success. Beethoven was obviously the best composer of his generation, and therefore the Grand Master, but Sibelius was not.

Having established that the world of classical music has been controlled since its inception by a mysterious order of musicians who have passed on the secret of musical creation from generation to generation, the only question was now: *how strongly connected with freemasonry is this musicians' secret order?* The answer appears to be: *very close.*

Indeed, the only separation between masons and musicians comes about through a religious influence which is in itself masonic if you regard the Knights Templar as juxtaposed to the masons – which is certainly far from a ridiculous notion.

Selecting the best composers (and therefore the Grand Masters) from each age was a relatively easy task, thanks to a helpful assistant in the classical music section of our local W. H. Smiths who gave estimates (of which we have no reason to doubt the accuracy) of the most popular compact discs in his shop.

The very first Grand Master seems to have been Guido d'Arezzo (990–1050), a Benedictine Monk who took musical notation to the kind of stage we would recognize today. (And there's the first link between religion and the formula for success.) D'Arezzo was followed swiftly by Perotin-le-Grand (1160–1220) who was in charge of music at the chapel whichstood where Notre-Dame now stands in Paris, and who developed polyphonic music *and its notation*!

An equation was beginning to formulate itself:

RELIGION + MUSIC + KNOWLEDGE OF NOTATION = POPULARITY!

BRANDENBURG-GATE

Maestro followed maestro as the hereditary line progressed through the centuries and crossed European boundaries.

In England the first Grand Master was a monk in Reading who composed the ever-popular 'Sumer is icumen in' and the less popular 'I is a coider drinker', before passing back the baton to France.

After Guillaume de Machaut (cf. *Pokergate*, p47) had dazzled the musical world with his brilliance, however, the good times stopped rolling and a darker aspect to the order's work became visible. The brilliant keyboard player and composer Cabezon (1510–1566) became blind! Why? We can only guess that he had broken the rules – written or unwritten. Or perhaps it was just one rule that he broke, and this is our thesis: *that the only thing that was forbidden by the order was that no Grand Master should rise above himself*. Why else should Mozart have been poisoned in 1756, Beethoven deafened in 1800 and Webern shot dead – allegedly by an 'American soldier' – in 1945?

But before we get to the twentieth century, think first of the English composer William Byrd. Here we find the strongest hint of the power of the order. As a Catholic in the latter part of the sixteenth century, Byrd found himself a religious outlaw in his own country. Yet, in 1575, he managed to secure from the Crown the monopoly for printing music in England!

How else can that be explained save for the dominant nature of the order – trouncing religious bigotry no less. Even Byrd's publication of catholic choral music at the time of the Gunpowder Plot (cf. *Traitor's Gate*, p57) failed to lead to the anti-papist backlash one might have expected. Indeed, that choral music included one ballad which became the most popular of its time, uniting Catholics and Protestants in celebrations which included complicated and absurd dance rituals. At every gathering, when those present had drunk a little too much, the cry would go up for a communal performance of 'Ye Byrdee Song'.

Freemasonry entered the order (as far as we can tell for the first time) in 1785 when Wolfgang Amadeus Mozart became

BRANDENBURG-GATE

Grand Master and a mason simultaneously. He seemed to run riot with his new-found secret for devising the perfect tune. His success was spiralling out of control when he was cruelly cut down. As we have suggested above, he broke the one big rule: never use the secret combinations of notes and harmonies to an extent which makes you *over*-popular. The same can be said of Beethoven, whose ability was lessened by being deafened. But what of Webern? He seemed in little danger of becoming over-popular, so why was he assassinated? Perhaps in his case it was not that he used the secret combinations of notes too much. He just decided to mix up the *order* of the notes. Such disrespect earned the ultimate retribution.

There have been no more such punishments in evidence since 1945 and let us hope there will be no more.

But remember the extract from the musical at the start of this chapter in which the notes were reversed? We did not name the composer, nor dare we, for such disrespect from the man who is clearly the current Grand Master would surely result in revenge of a truly dreadful nature were the order ever to note it. If they *do* realize that, not only is their Grand Master becoming *too* successful, he is also writing the code phrases backwards, we urge forgiveness. He is, after all, an ugly man who has to live with that disadvantage every day of his life. Has he not suffered enough?

Suffragate
or
NOT ONLY FOOLS AND HORSES

We now felt ready to tackle that most scandalous of all eras – our own. Surely though (one might ask) everything that is worth knowing about in the twentieth century is already out in the open, such is the pace of technological development that leaves no stone unturned in its wake? Not necessarily.

Who would have thought, for example, that deep in the bowels of the Caxton Advertising Agency – used by the War Office for recruitment campaigns since 1913 – we'd find the original artwork for the poster which was to make Lord Kitchener a household moustache?

Wouldn't even more of the nation's gilded youth have signed up to go 'over the top' in the Great War if the powers that be had had the courage of their convictions? Nobody will ever know. But we were excited enough to start delving deeper into the century of the common man – and the not-so-common woman...

Unsolved to this day is the mystery of why Emily Davison became the first recorded person ever to invade a pitch: in this case the Derby course at Epsom

SUFFRAGATE

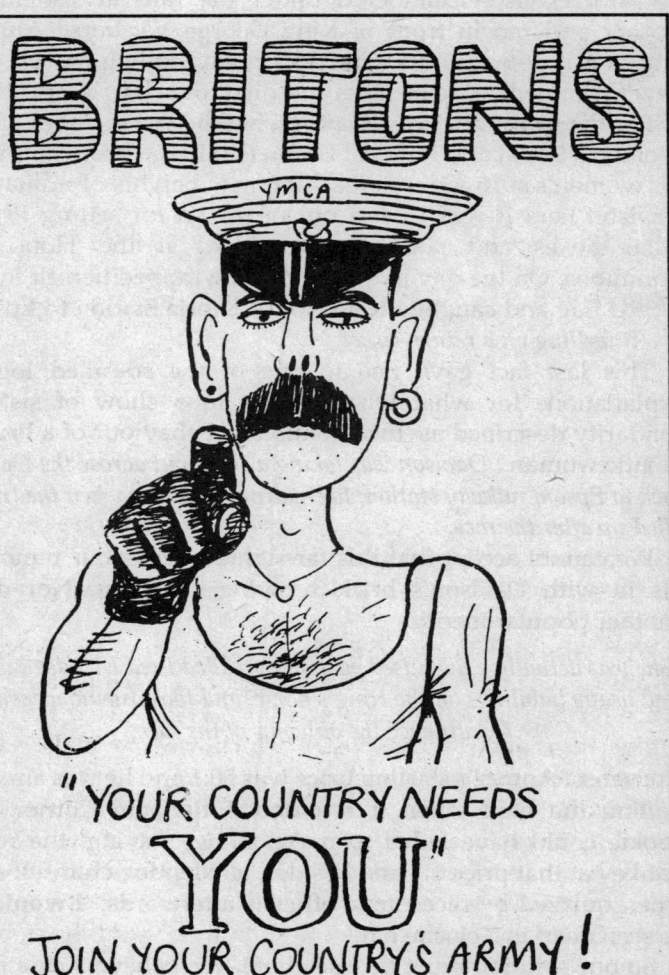

SUFFRAGATE

in 1913. Davison clambered under the rails at Tattenham Corner and ran in front of King George V's horse Anmer: bringing it down, injuring the jockey and killing herself (she never regained consciousness and died four days later).

For the last seven years Davison had been a member of the Women's Social and Political Union (WSPU) whose campaign for women's suffrage was reaching new heights of militancy: Davison herself was in and out of prison for setting fire to pillar boxes and smashing windows at the House of Commons. On the day in question she wrapped herself in the WSPU flag and caught a train from Victoria Station to Epsom ... *travelling on a return ticket.*

This last fact gave rise to one of the so-called logical explanations for what Queen Mary in a show of sisterly solidarity described as 'the abominable behaviour of a brutal, lunatic woman': *Davison was taking a short-cut across the Downs back to Epsom railway station, to ensure a good seat when the trains filled up after the race.*

We cannot accept that this far-sighted behaviour remotely fits in with Davison's brick-throwing character. Nor does another popular theory:

> *She was actually a disguised bookmaker called Fred Mendoza who had heavy liabilities on the King's horse, and took drastic measures to influence the outcome of the race.*

Nonsense! Anmer's starting price was 50:1 and he was already trailing the field when it rounded Tattenham Corner. No bookie could have failed to make money 'laying' the royal donkey at that price ... and besides, as Mendoza himself said when quizzed by racecourse officials afterwards, 'I wouldn't be seen dead in a cloche hat.'

So our solution must lie elsewhere. We believe a clue is to be found in an eye-witness report given by one St. John Ervine, reported in the *Daily Mail*:

> 'Miss Davison, who was standing close to the rails a few yards from me, suddenly ducked under the

railings as the King's horse came up ... she cried "Votes For Women!" and put up her hand, but whether it was to catch hold of the reins or to protect herself, I do not know.'

We think Mr St John Ervine *did* know. For a start, he was not just a common-or-garden punter standing in the Tattersalls enclosure: he was the celebrated Belfast author of several plays about the Troubles in Northern Ireland!

So what was he doing in England on that June day? It is surely no coincidence that the subject of Home Rule for Ireland was currently a Parliamentary hot potato, with the Liberal Government relying on the votes of its Irish supporters to keep it in power.

The Prime Minister, Herbert Asquith, and his Chancellor and right-hand man, David Lloyd George, would have been taking soundings and expert advice from interested parties, St John Ervine included. It may well have been at this time that Asquith got wind of Lloyd George's long-term plan to replace him as Prime Minister (which eventually happened in 1916).

And it is our theory, based on our knowledge of human nature and the recollections of our grandfathers (both of whom knew Lloyd George) that Asquith and his supporters hatched the idea of an unholy Liberal alliance with the WSPU. The express intention of this plot was nothing less than to ruin the career of the Chancellor of the Exchequer.

Lloyd George's weakness for women was well known. Let us suppose there was a meeting between the Prime Minister or his representatives and the Suffragettes. (There is no evidence whatsoever that such a meeting ever took place, but as experience has constantly taught us, this does not mean it did not happen.)

It might well have been suggested to Emmeline Pankhurst and her cohorts that if they were to oblige Lloyd George in his whims, be liberal with their favours in fact, he would

SUFFRAGATE

accommodate them in their wish for emancipation . . . a technique to become known as 'the voting couch'.

That this plan was at least partially put into operation is supported by the appearance of Mrs Pankhurst in court early in 1913. She was charged with bombing Lloyd George's country villa at Walton Heath – the classic act of a jilted woman. It is highly probable that she had set herself up in the Chancellor's stables, under the soubriquet 'Miss Horsewhip' or some such, and her true intentions had only been revealed when she filed tax returns under her real name.

But what of Emily Davison? Clearly she was the plan's second stage. It's our belief that she infiltrated herself into Number 11 Downing Street, in the role of cook. Lloyd George duly succumbed to her charms . . . but not her cooking. Catering for a husband was a duty the feminist Davison had steadfastly refused to take up, with the result that the official meals she prepared were pronounced 'not fragrant' by more than one important visiting financier.

Davison was dismissed. Spurned, she started breaking windows at the House of Commons, and sending blackmail demands to Lloyd George through the post . . . then thinking better of it and trying to set fire to the pillar box. One of these (and this is still, be it remembered, only supposition) reached the Chancellor's office.

Lloyd George panicked and turned for help to his new friend St John Ervine. The playwright came to the rescue – on condition that the Government allowed the counties that formed Ulster the chance to opt out of the Home Rule proposals. Lloyd George agreed, and gave St John Ervine £20 in a brown envelope (the equivalent of £2,000 at today's rates) to pay Davison off.

They arranged to meet at Victoria Station. Unfortunately St John Ervine misunderstood the telephoned instructions: he took 'I'll be wearing a flag' to mean that Davison would have a *fag* in her mouth – women smoking in public being at that time a distinctive phenomenon. But he was in time to see her boarding the train to Epsom: Davison had always meant to go there to spend her ill-gotten gains by having a flutter on the Derby.[1]

The rest of the story is of course self-evident. St John Ervine followed Davison on to the course and was still trying to press Lloyd George's money on her when the race started. Overcome by loyalty to her cause she refused, warding off the playwright with her raised hand and a contemptuous cry of 'Notes for Quimmin!' – a vulgar Chaucerian reference to the sexual act much favoured by these proto-Women's Libbers.

With Emily Davison out of harm's way in the mortuary there was no need for Lloyd George to keep his bargain with St John Ervine – and the troubles in Northern Ireland continue to this day. The sordid chain of events was summarised by St John Ervine in a neat phrase which has also survived the passage of time: 'The Cock-Up Theory of History'.

A contemporary children's toy, a precursor of today's 'Snow-Shakers'

[1] Ironically, Davison intended to back the King's horse – even Suffragettes had the women's weakness for anything with a royal connection!

SUFFRAGATE

> ### INTERESTING FOOTNOTE
>
> *   Aboyeur, a complete outsider, won the Derby.
> ** Women gct the vote five years later.
> *** A 'Double' on the above two events would have paid over 3,000:1.

Fattygate

One of Hollywood's most tragic figures was the comedian Roscoe 'Fatty' Arbuckle, whose hitherto rocketing career never recovered from his foolish involvement with a starlet. Though acquitted of all charges, 'The Minister of Slapstick Arts' was a ruined man. He could be seen haunting the studio back-lots for years afterwards, occasionally contributing material to comedy films at the invitation of his few loyal friends, and writing features on the arts, opera and lotteries for the *Los Angeles Times*.

Of the many who may have passed by on the other side, none was more celebrated than Charlie Chaplin – and recently some strange rumours (we dare put them no higher than that) have been in circulation that throw startling new light on the competitive relationship between the two men, and indeed the whole history of the cinema.

For this theory (and it must be stressed again that it *is* only a theory) we are indebted to those engaged on research for Roman Polanski's film of the life of Chaplin – a project unfortunately still-born when the Richard Attenborough version went into production. The *Chaplin* according to Polanski was expected to concentrate much more on the actor/writer/director/composer's sex life, in particular his sometimes dangerous liking for the company of girls who (shall we say) didn't yet have their driving licence.

FATTYGATE

Fatty on the other hand liked them skinny, and his eye soon fell on the aspiring actress Virginia Rappe. Offering to put her into his next picture, he also took a small apartment where they met after the day's work. Virginia confessed to friends that she was turned on by the sense of power that associating with one of Hollywood's big names gave her. Then there was Fatty's sense of fun: when feeling especially fruity he would dress up in the strip of his favourite team, the Boston Red Sox.

Virginia was more coy about her lover's sexual proclivities, but did reveal that he was fond of biting her toes, sometimes being so overcome with passion that he didn't even take her shoes off first!

What really happened that night in 1921 remains a mystery. Fatty had taken her into his suite at the St. Francis Hotel in San Francisco during a wild Labor Day party, with a wink and the words, 'This is the chance I've waited for for a long time.'

FATTYGATE

Was it also the chance somebody else had been waiting for?

We know that at the time Fatty Arbuckle was a star as big as if not bigger than Charlie Chaplin. We also know that Chaplin was enormously ambitious, and years ahead of his time in his thinking about the cinema and its possibilities.

Perhaps Virginia wasn't the 'wannabe' she pretended – it could have been a brilliant act, coaxed out of her by a master director. Perhaps it was always intended that she should go into that room with Fatty, knowing that it was 'bugged' – with hidden cameras and perhaps even a pioneering form of sound recording equipment.

In which case the 'buggers' picked up more than they bargained for, as Virginia's laughter turned to screams and she perished under the weight of the 19-stone Arbuckle (or 20 if you include his shoulder and shin pads).

Hastily the room next door would have been cleared of its blackmailing paraphernalia. Everything including the cameras – and the experimental sound system – would have been dumped into the San Francisco Bay as the conspirators fled the scandal and high-tailed it back down the coast to Hollywood. It would be five years before the first 'talkie' – the makers of Al Jolson's *The Jazz Singer* taking the credit for another fruit of Chaplin's fertile brain.

Of course this remains sheer conjecture – apart from one telling footnote (literally): the famous scene in the film *The Gold Rush* where a desperate Charlie Chaplin first cooks then EATS HIS SHOES.

Could this be a deliberate mocking reference to the sexual tastes of his former chum?

Harrgate

Agatha Christie was called many things in her time: 'Queen of Crime', 'Dame Commander of the British Empire', 'author', etc. But it was not until we chanced upon a reference to her in the *Daily Mirror*'s library of GCHQ Royal Transcripts (1950–59) that we came to discover Christie's *real* name. The Government snoopers had apparently picked up a snippet of a phone conversation made from an extension in the Buckingham Palace Long Gallery on 24th November 1952. The transcript reads as follows:

WOMAN: Hello. Mayfair 0500.

INDETERMINATE: Hello – is that MI5?

WOMAN: Yes.

INDETERMINATE: Extension 3 please.

WOMAN: May I say who's calling?

INDETERMINATE: Just say it's the Fourth Man stroke First Woman.

WOMAN: Trying to connect you, Mrs Christie.

[*Pause*]

MAN: Hello, Agatha.

INDETERMINATE: Hello, Major. May I see you this week?

MAN: How about tomorrow night?

INDETERMINATE: No can do. First night of *The Mousetrap*.

MAN: Oh, now do tell me . . . who done it?

HARROGATE

(Tape breaks up due to interference)

What could this mean? What was Agatha Christie doing in the Long Gallery of Buckingham Palace? Why was she in touch with MI5? Was she a spy?

There was only one place to start the search for the answers to these particular questions – Christie's novels. The clues we unearthed from those 'whodunits' soon crystallized into a startling conjecture which proved once more that truth can be *much* stranger than fiction!

On 27 May 1926 Agatha Christie's *The Murder of Roger Ackroyd* was published and became a popular and controversial bestseller. The twist of having the narrator as murderer was hailed as ingenious and original. The novel was serialized in the *Daily News* and her future seemed assured. But then she disappeared!

On the night of the 4 December 1926, Agatha Christie drove away from her home ('Styles') and vanished into thin air. A nationwide man-hunt ensued and – after the *Daily News* put up a reward of £100 for information leading to the discovery of her whereabouts – she was *apparently* found in a hotel in Harrogate on 13 December.

Apparently? Yes, apparently, because the true story of what happened to Agatha Christie has never been told. Until now. Rumour at the time of Christie's disappearance had it that her husband's alleged affair with a Miss Neele of Godalming was the trigger for her flight. Certainly the marriage between the author and Colonel Archibald Christie did not survive many months after they were reunited at the Hydro Hotel in Harrogate. Why?

Neither the colonel nor his wife would make any statement after she had been found. Why?

The books that appeared in the years to come under the name of Agatha Christie sold in their millions around the globe. Why?

HARROGATE

To answer these questions one must start by stating the obvious truth.

THE 'WOMAN' 'FOUND' IN HARROGATE WAS NOT AGATHA CHRISTIE!

A shocking statement. So's this:

AGATHA CHRISTIE WAS MURDERED AND IMPERSONATED UNTIL HER 'DEATH' IN 1976 BY SOMEONE ELSE!

Let's start by looking at the build-up to Harrogate.

Christie's first novel, *The Mysterious Affair at Styles*, was published in 1920. More 'whodunits' followed and a series of stories appeared in the magazine *Sketch*. What all this work revealed – apart from an ability to tell a detective story efficiently – was an acute, deep-seated loathing of servants; in particular, butlers. It was invariably the butler who 'did it' and this was noticed in England by the real-life butlers themselves.

Resentment at being pilloried week after week in *Sketch*, and in every novel Christie wrote, was increasing below stairs when 1926 arrived. In January of that year, the senior fiction editor of Collins the publishers was reading the manuscript of *The Murder of Roger Ackroyd* at home and foolishly left it in his study overnight, where his butler found it. He was horrified to read the following extracts (which his master was in the process of toning down) concerning the fictitious butler, Parker:

CHAPTER 4

I was surprised to find Parker just outside. He seemed rather embarrassed, and I wondered for a moment whether he had perhaps been listening at the door, as these deceitful cretins who serve us so often do.

What a plump, conceited, greasy face the man

HARROGATE

had, and there was definitely something suspicious in the demeanour of this non-person . . . this louse . . . this insult to mankind.

Chapter 5

Suddenly, the sound of a rattling chain disturbed me and I found Parker, his imperturbable expression still in place, blocking the open doorway. The man looked more repugnant than ever. I did not even bother to speak as I pushed past him into the hall. Why bother to waste one's breath on a member of a subspecies?

Predictably, it was going to be the butler who had 'dunit' once more. The clues were there to see:

Chapter 6

[Inspector Davis:] 'I've been making some enquiries as to what Parker has been up to this evening. I have to say, I don't trust the man. He knows more than he's telling. When I started to ask questions, he told me a cock-and-bull tale about blackmail. But he's obviously the murderer.

'I just need twenty-four hours to sweat the bastard. Let me beat the truth out of the servile swine.'

It was too much for the real butler to bear and he took the manuscript to a hastily convened meeting of the Mayfair chapter of the League of Gentlemen's Gentlemen (LOGG) that very night. They agreed that enough was enough and a message was immediately conveyed to Agatha Christie via her own manservant (Trotter) that her life would be terminated unless she rewrote *The Murder of Roger Ackroyd* with Parker as hero, and never penned an insulting word against servants again. In effect, the Gentlemen's Gentlemen had issued a Fatwa's Fatwa.

Christie refused to take this threat seriously, but Collins did. The senior fiction editor listened to his own butler's calm assertion that their best-selling author was about to be disposed of and rewrote *The Murder of Roger Ackroyd* himself – taking out the more extreme criticism of Parker and cobbling together the surprise (and quite ludicrous) ending so that the narrator became the killer.

Christie was furious when she saw the final proofs and stormed round to the editor's house to confront him. The butler answered the door and, as usual, was treated to a torrent of abuse from the author. He in turn repeated the threat to her life which Trotter had passed on, and something in the servant's demeanour told Christie she really was in danger. She rushed to the police and demanded protection.

A meeting of senior detectives at Scotland Yard was convened and arrangements for armed guards to accompany Christie everywhere were made . . . on one condition: in future novels, there were to be no more Belgian detectives helping the British police with their enquiries. This was too much for Christie to bear and on the night of 4th December she went into hiding with the death threat still hanging over her.

Arriving in Harrogate she checked into the Hydro Hotel and set about insulting any servant who came within shouting distance. Naturally, she was quickly recognized by a chamber maid who informed the local chapter of LOGG that their quarry was installed in Room 101. A hit-squad – armed with a candlestick, a rope, a revolver and a Moroccan dagger – went to the hotel and murdered Agatha Christie. The crime was reported to the police when the butlers had made their getaway and the detectives from Scotland Yard who just hours before had been discussing her protection arrived to examine the body.

They were in a dilemma. If news of the death of the most popular novelist in the country leaked out, the police would be blamed for not preventing her murder. But how could they conceal the crime?

It took just nine days for the most elaborate and successful cover-up of the century to be formulated, and on 13 December 1926 'Agatha Christie' reappeared.

Who was she? To answer that, we must go to Marlborough, where a boy aged nineteen was about to go up to Trinity College, Cambridge. His name? Anthony Blunt.

For over a decade now, it has been accepted that Anthony Blunt was one of four traitors who betrayed their country (the others, of course, being Burgess, Maclean and Philby). But in actual fact, Blunt was a hero who risked his life for more than half a century as a *triple*, not a double, agent.

When Christie was killed, the then Deputy Head of the Security Service (Major Metcalf) saw a chance to put into play a plan he'd devised some months earlier – one of the most complicated deceptions conceivable and the first known use of a so-called 'sleeper'.

Metcalf had spotted the young, rather beautiful Blunt at Marlborough and recognized that the boy would almost certainly drift into the world of espionage, communism and betrayal. He made the boy an offer: work for the British, but when approached by the Russians, pretend to work for them too.

Blunt was tempted but couldn't see what was in it for him. Metcalf wanted to offer him large sums of money but the Service just didn't have a budget for such a long-term project. Then, when Christie was killed, Metcalf seized his chance – Blunt could pretend to be the author, which would not only guarantee years of enormous royalty cheques but would also give Blunt the opportunity to dress up as a woman at weekends and on public holidays.

The deal was done and Anthony became Agatha. Naturally, Colonel Christie was far from happy about sharing his bed with a schoolboy and sued for divorce. Being the loyal soldier he was, however, he kept the subterfuge a secret and never told a soul what had happened. (Nothing queer about Colonel Christie.)

HARROGATE

Blunt succeeded in combining his studies with the straightforward task of churning out 'whodunits'. After Cambridge, he joined MI5 having (as predicted) been recruited by the Russians. The help he gave in minimizing the damage done by Philby etc. can only be guessed at and it is a wonder that he kept up the constant flow of thrillers whilst serving two masters in the world of secret intelligence. However, his editor at Collins (who was kept in the dark) did notice occasional lapses in style when Blunt let his imagination carry him away. The following extract from the original manuscript of *Murder On The Orient Express* is indicative of the type of passage which had to be amended:

CHAPTER 1

> *Dawn was breaking in Syria. At Aleppo station stood the Taurus Express, with its kitchen, dining-car, sleeping-car and two local coaches.*
>
> *Next to the steps which led up to the sleeping-car stood a young Italian lieutenant, radiant in uniform, his firm thighs straining the seams of his jodhpurs. The soldier was a Greek god in comparison to the small Belgian detective he was kissing. As Poirot fought to escape the passionate embrace in which he was held, pressed hard against the side of the train, he felt a hand slide beneath his heavy over-coat and grasp his . . .*
> [ILLEGIBLE]

Blunt enjoyed inserting jokes about his friends and colleagues into his novels. Hence the character who opens *The Sittaford Mystery* is called Major BURNABY – BUR from BURgess; NA from MacleAN (the final two letters reversed); and BY from PhilBY. In *The Mousetrap* he even penned an exact description of ex–lover Guy Burgess (who had just fled to Russia – hence the over-night bag):

HARROGATE

ACT I
SCENE 1

[*MR PARAVICINI enters up R, holding an overnight bag. He is dark and very old with an ostentatious moustache and a pronounced limp.*]

Of course, Blunt also enjoyed a highly successful career as an art historian, for which he dressed as a man. In fact he seemed to thrive on the 'split personality' his lifestyle demanded and, in 1930, he (as Agatha) married Max Mallowan the archaeologist. He (as Anthony) was appointed Surveyor of the King's Pictures in 1945 and kept up an impressive output of academic and fictitious work almost until his death: in 1950 Blunt wrote a series of monographs on the Royal collections, a highly praised volume on French art and architecture, major works on Italian baroque and rococo architecture and *A Murder Is Announced*.

Agatha Christie

Anthony Blunt

He was knighted in 1956 and became a Dame in 1971. At which point things started to go wrong.

Major Metcalf had long since passed away, leaving no one in MI5 (or indeed the Government) privy to the true identity of Agatha Christie. Blunt was getting old and tired. He couldn't be bothered to keep writing fiction and his final novel (*Postern of Fate*) was published in 1974, when he also stepped down as Director of the Courtauld Institute.

In 1976, Harold Wilson resigned and Blunt decided Agatha should also depart the scene: he announced 'her' death.

All might have ended happily had not Margaret Thatcher been elected in 1979. She instigated further investigation of the Secret Intelligence Service and when a 'confession' signed by Blunt in 1964 came to light, she exposed him in the House of Commons.

The confession had, of course, been yet one more piece in the jigsaw of deception which had kept Burgess, Maclean and Philby ignorant of the fact that *they* were the ones who had been duped. No one believed Blunt's story that he'd been a triple agent (let alone Agatha Christie) and he suffered public humiliation. He was stripped of his knighthood (but kept his posthumous damehood) and died in 1983. Only now can we pay tribute, not only to the most secret of secret agents this country has ever had, but also to the finest transvestite ever to write a 'whodunit'!

Abdigate

Noël 'the Master' Coward was famed as a writer, actor, lyricist and suave man-about-town ... what is less well known is that when returning to his London flat in the small hours, he was often so full of beans that he sat up till breakfast-time playing with his 'ham' radio.

As this contemporary caricature shows, Coward would roam the airwaves, sharing the unguarded moments of lonely merchant seamen crossing the Channel. One night he seems to have picked up more than he bargained for – a conversation of

ABDIGATE

the gravest national and constitutional importance. Being a celebrated West End playwright, of course, Coward was most interested in it as material for some future comedy . . . and indeed his notes show that these intimate moments eventually made their way into *Private Lives*:

EDWARD: . . . so terribly, terribly dear, and sweet, and attractive, and . . .

WALLIS: Oh do stop, David. We must talk about the practicalities.

EDWARD: Yes, you're right. You're so terribly, terribly right, and sweet, and attractive, and . . .

WALLIS: Your speech, David. Have you drafted your speech yet?

EDWARD: I've been having a few problems, actually. You know I'm not very good with words, Wallis.

WALLIS: You're better than your brother. Half a sentence from him and the floor's wet. And you said such clever things in Wales last month.

EDWARD: Oh, my 'Something Must Be Done' slogan. That took weeks to write.

WALLIS: Did you compose it all by yourself?

EDWARD: No, I got some help from the Duke of Norfolk.

WALLIS: Very fat, Norfolk.

EDWARD: No, he's not.

WALLIS: Are you contradicting me, honey? I've a good mind to press button B.

EDWARD: I wish you were pressing my button B, harder and harder.

WALLIS: I'd have to find it first.

ABDIGATE

EDWARD: Oh, darling Wallis. I do so want to . . . erm . . . fill your tank.

WALLIS: Whatever can you mean, David?

EDWARD: You know . . . er . . . sort of, well, be with you . . . inside your plus-fours, actually.

WALLIS: Don't be so revolting. Besides, I'm wearing a cocktail dress.

EDWARD: Just my luck. Oh, I wish I were dead, then perhaps I could come back as a pair of your cami-knickers.

WALLIS: Don't talk such rot. We really must work on your abdication speech. What are you going to say?

EDWARD: Well, I . . . erm . . . that is . . .

WALLIS: Do you have some paper and a pen?

EDWARD: Yes. I wish I were the paper in your smallest room.

WALLIS: Shut up. Take this down: 'At long last . . . '

EDWARD: 'At . . . long . . . last . . . '

WALLIS: 'I am able to say a few words . . . '

EDWARD: ' . . . a . . . few . . . words . . . '

WALLIS: 'Of my own.'

EDWARD: 'Of . . . my . . . ' Dash it. I've run out of ink.

[Transcript is interrupted while Coward pours himself a cocktail and fits a new wax cylinder in his recording equipment]

EDWARD: . . . 'must believe me when I tell you that I have found it impossible to carry the heavy burden of responsibility and to discharge my duties as King as I would wish to do without the help and support of the woman I love. You see, love is no use unless it's wise and

ABDIGATE

kind, steady and sweet, to smooth out one's nerves when one is tired.' You don't think this is too dull do you Wallis?

[*Faint snoring can be heard*]

EDWARD: Wallis!

WALLIS: Oh! What is it?

EDWARD: Don't you think it goes on rather?

WALLIS: Well, cut out the bit at the end. But don't forget to bless everyone and do a 'God Save The King'.

EDWARD: Won't that be a bit self-reverential?

WALLIS: Not by then.

EDWARD: Oh no. Are you happy?

WALLIS: Perfectly. Are you?

EDWARD: Ecstatically. [*Yawns*]

WALLIS: You're exhausted. You must go to sleep now, darling.

EDWARD: Yes, darling. I do love you, you know. And I'm so proud of you.

WALLIS: Don't be silly. I've never achieved anything.

EDWARD: Yes you have.

WALLIS: No I haven't.

EDWARD: Your great achievement is to have plunged the British monarchy into a constitutional crisis whilst appearing immune to all the indignities and tortures and calumnies.

[*Pause*]

EDWARD: Night night, darling.

ABDIGATE

WALLIS: Good night.

EDWARD: Au revoir.

WALLIS: Night.

EDWARD: Cheero.

WALLIS: Night.

EDWARD: Toodle-pip.

WALLIS: [*Yawning*] Good night.

EDWARD: Love you. Nighty-night.

WALLIS: Night, David.

EDWARD: Wallis?

WALLIS: Oh, what is it?

EDWARD: I hope you won't mind me asking . . .

WALLIS: Well?

EDWARD: But, why do you call me David when my name's Edward?

[WALLIS *screams silently*]

   [*The phone is replaced on its hook and the transcript ends*]

LAMP POST gate

Benito Mussolini was a man who flirted with danger throughout his life. In 1919 he formed the Fasci di Combattimento (which translates roughly as 'Dangerous Sports Club') and was voted chairman for life, taking the title 'Il Duce'. With their distinctive black sports shirts, Mussolini's fun-loving fascists would often take to the streets looking for something risky to do – sometimes kidnapping communists just for the hell of it. Il Duce himself was almost killed four or five times, once when he dared the Hon. Violet Gibson to see how close she could fire a bullet to his nose: she hit it! The rest of the fascists thought Benito had divine protection and were keen for him to play in goal in the 1934 World Cup final in Rome (Italy vs. Czechoslovakia). Sadly, a knee injury kept him out of the game but the Italians won 2–1 none the less.

Discussions with Adolf Hitler in 1938 gave Mussolini a whole new set of ideas for dangerous games involving piano wire but the Second World War forced him to postpone the festival of risky sports which he had envisaged putting on in the Coliseum. Instead, he concentrated on bullying the rail unions into running an efficient train service. They took such treatment in bad humour and vowed vengeance. Their opportunity knocked in 1945.

LAMPPOSTGATE

Concerned by the country's morale, Mussolini decided to introduce a new activity which would entertain the public and provide him with the thrills he still sought: bungee jumping! Taking along his mistress, Clara Petacci, Il Duce found a vacant lamppost and climbed to the top. Attaching what he thought was an elastic cord to his ankles he launched himself into midair – relishing the cheers of the watching crowd. Sadly for him, the rail union shop stewards had substituted the elastic with extra strong garden twine.

The rest is history.

Lillibetgate

In 1933 Miss Marion Crawford joined the Royal Household as nursery governess to Princess Elizabeth and Princess Margaret Rose. She was known throughout her working life as 'Crawfie' and not only taught and looked after the 'two little girls' (as she called them) but also became the then Queen-to-be's closest associate.

Crawfie brings up the rear

Crawfie was privy to all the secrets of the young Royals and accompanied them to every formal, and most informal, occasions right up until Princess Elizabeth became engaged to the Duke of Edinburgh (as he is now known).

LILLIBETGATE

In her retirement, Crawfie not only hoped for a substantial pension and 'grace-and-favour' cottage, but also for the honour of being appointed Dame Commander of the Victorian Order. This was not to be. The New Year Honours lists of 1947, 1948 and 1949 were published without the inclusion of Marion Crawford's name and so she decided to seek her revenge: finding no interest amongst the Fleet Street editors in a leaked copy of George VI's 1949 Christmas Message to the Nation, she decided to publish her memoirs!

It is hard in this day and age fully to comprehend the shock to the Establishment, and to the country as a whole, which Crawfie's action delivered. But in 1950 it was unheard of for a Royal servant to vouchsafe *any* detail of life with the Bowes-Lyons (let alone the Windsors).

And yet *MARGARET: Her True Story. (And Lillibet's Too)* – to use Crawfie's preferred title for the book which eventually appeared as *The Little Princesses* – was a tame, not to say dull, diary recording the day-to-day activities of the young Royals. There was no salacious gossip, so why such a strong reaction from the Palace? (They refused ever again to even mention Crawfie's name and immediately tightened the rules restricting what former employees could disclose to the public.)

The answer can at last be revealed.

We were fortunate to be granted access to what the anonymous vendor assured us was the original manuscript submitted by Marion Crawford. And the blue pencil marks tell their own story!

Who can doubt that word got back to Princess Elizabeth about what had been deleted from the final proofs, and who can wonder at the then future Queen's anger over what *might* have been revealed to the general public?

LILLIBETGATE

PENGUIN BOOKS

MARGARET

HER TRUE STORY

(And Lilibet's Too)

MARION CRAWFORD

COMPLETE 2/6 UNABRIDGED

LILLIBETGATE

(The extracts from Crawfie's diary they refused to publish.)

10TH DECEMBER 1933 – 145 PICCADILLY

Margaret Rose is talking more and more, bless her. Such a bright and gay child – quite unlike Lillibet, whose demeanour becomes more serious each day. M so wants to call her sister by the pet name we all use but Lillibet insists she refer to her as 'Ma'am'!

14TH AUGUST 1934

Some gentlemen from the press were gathered outside Hamilton Gardens as we took our morning stroll today. M was keen to pose for the photographers in the bright sunshine despite L's protestations. Imagine my surprise when M suddenly lifted her skirt to show off her new knickers! Still, the press are honourable men who will not, I am sure, print such a revealing photograph.

7TH NOVEMBER 1934

L is becoming increasingly annoyed at the attention M is getting from the public as we wander through Mayfair. Everyone wants to admire the younger Princess and the applause from gathered crowds is certainly more voluble when M, rather than L, returns their waves.

23RD JANUARY 1935

I have had to give Margaret Rose a severe ticking off. This morning I caught her riding her bicycle down the corridor with the wind-up gramophone strapped to her waist. She told me this was so she could enjoy the music wherever she went. I was forced to slap her wrist. Whatever next?

3RD MARCH 1935

Oh dear. M has decided she doesn't like Bobo, the nursery maid, and insists she be dismissed. L loves Bobo and won't let her go, so the two little girls are at loggerheads once more. This year has already seen the departure of two detectives: L

LILLIBETGATE

claims they were always giving sweets to M and were over-familiar. It is hard for anyone to resist the charms of Margaret Rose when she looks up from beneath her fringe with those big brown eyes.

12TH MAY 1937 – BUCKINGHAM PALACE

Coronation Day, and I fear the excitement of the occasion affected Margaret quite badly. She was sick three times this morning and twice in the afternoon. Still, she tried her best to overcome her nerves, and Cook found her in the kitchen after supper helping herself to custard, ice cream, cold chicken and pickle! Good to know her appetite is as healthy as ever, though Heaven knows where she puts it all – she's as thin as a rake!

27TH DECEMBER 1938 – WINDSOR CASTLE

What a surprise at the pantomime tonight! As usual, the girls had little roles to perform with members of the Household in the gay entertainment they give us every Christmas (*Cinderella* this year). Just as the first act was finishing, I noticed that M had left the chorus line and was nowhere to be seen on stage. Imagine how thrilled we were when a drum roll heralded the dramatic entrance of Margaret Rose held aloft by Napp, the diminutive footman with the peculiar walk. A display of ballet followed, quite unlike any dance I'd seen before. The audience clapped and cheered, as did the cast – except for Lillibet who had a face like thunder. Oh dear. I do wish the girls were a little more friendly. They do squabble so.

2ND SEPTEMBER 1939 – BALMORAL

We are about to go to war with Germany. The King and Queen returned to London this afternoon and there was a dreadful mood of depression throughout the castle. Lillibet did her best to cheer us all up with amusing impersonations of characters from her favourite radio programme, *There's That Man Again* (or some such nonsense). I do wish Margaret Rose would at least *pretend* to find her sister funny.

LILLIBETGATE

30TH OCTOBER 1939 – BIRKHALL
I have banned M's friend, Sarah, from playing here ever again. Larking about in Girl Guide uniforms is one thing but what they did to Ruby was unforgivable: umbrellas are dangerous things and the poor girl may be scarred for life.

4TH MARCH 1940 – WINDSOR CASTLE
Margaret Rose is in a mood. She overheard Lillibet chatting to Owen (the groom) in the yard. She is very cross, having believed that L was no longer on speaking terms with the young lad. I am sure it is a purely innocent friendship: they simply share a passion for horses. M insists L should never see Owen again and will sulk until she gets her way. (The little Madam!)

7TH MARCH 1940
Oh dear. Margaret Rose fell down the stairs this morning, crashing into a glass cabinet at the bottom and cutting her wrist quite badly. She has become very accident-prone of late – how she managed to gash her finger with the lemon slicer I shall never know.

15TH JULY 1941
Day in, day out, M will not leave her sick hamster's side. She dotes on the poor creature and smothers it with love and affection. What a contrast to her treatment of poor Lillibet last week who sprained her wrist falling off a pony. Sympathy seemed in *very* short supply then!

7TH AUGUST 1941
Oh dear. Margaret Rose has been crying for two days now. She cut her hair *very* short on Wednesday and, when Lillibet refused to say whether she liked it or not, she simply burst into tears and nothing will stem the tide!

8TH SEPTEMBER 1941
I do not believe it! This morning a photographer from a

LILLIBETGATE

national newspaper took a picture of L and M *without first asking permission*. Whatever next? It was particularly unfortunate since the two little girls were having a wee tiff at the time. (Not an unusual state of affairs these days!)

10TH SEPTEMBER 1941

Now the little girls have got us *all* at each others' throats! They want us to say which one of them we prefer, and we're not allowed to be friends with both! Lillibet has Allah, Bobo, Ruby and Cook on her side; M has Mr Fitch (the detective), Napp, and her imaginary companions Halifax, Pinkle Ponkle and Inderbombanks. I, of course, remain neutral. There is good in both of them but, oh dear – they do have their imperfections: M takes far too much trouble with her appearance for my liking, and L is always late for meals because she insists on helping the gardeners. One can take this 'Dig for Victory' business too seriously, in my opinion.

11TH SEPTEMBER 1941

As I feared, Margaret Rose has insisted on having her own bedroom. She claims Lillibet snores and keeps the light on too late in order to read. I suppose they are of an age now when they should have their privacy at night-time, and perhaps the constant bickering will subside, but I do think it's a shame when two young people who were once so close drift apart like this. Still, Lillibet is taking quite an interest in the blond Greek boy. So perhaps this is the start of a much happier era altogether!

INTERESTING FOOTNOTE

After the publication of *MARGARET: Her True Story. (And Lillibet's Too)*, the Establishment closed ranks behind the Royal Family and Crawfie was shunned whenever she tried to re-enter Society. Forced to spend her later years living in reduced circumstances, she took to peddling increasingly lurid and imaginative recollections. Worse, she did so in the gutter press, as this small ad from a 1950s edition of *Reveille* shows:

> **CRAWFIE CONFIDENTIAL!**
>
> Call me on FRObisher 2424 for the latest Inside Info
> on
> Right Royal Romps from:
>
> * Windsor 'Bouncy' Castle
> * Immoral Balmoral
> * ... and 'Buck' House itself
>
> Calls cost 2/6d peak times, 1/3d others
>
> **THEN TRY THESE ON FOR SIZE!**
> FRObisher 2425–"Your Obedient Servant!"
> FRObisher 2426–"Bareskins at the Barracks!"
> FRObisher 2427–"Come Kiss My Corgi!"
>
>

HOOVERGATE

THE CIA? THE MAFIA? THE INDUSTRIAL–MILITARY COMPLEX? A JILTED LOVER OF MARILYN MONROE JEALOUS OF HER RELATIONSHIP WITH THE PRESIDENT?

Four of the many byzantine conspiracy theories jostling to be taken seriously as the real motive for the assassination of John F. Kennedy. All, as far as we are concerned, arrant nonsense. The truth as we see it is much more straightforward, can be ascribed a simple human motive and – most important of all – can be laid at the door of one single person.

Lee Harvey Oswald.

Unfashionable, of course. But then so was the idea that a pork pie with a hard-boiled egg in it could be successfully marketed.

Once.

Why then, do we pin our colours so firmly to the mast of the much-reviled Warren Commission Report, widely seen to be a grotesque cover-up?

Of one thing we can be certain – a cover-up there was. And it still continues: in our submission every one of the theories listed above is but another smokescreen, a kind of relay race of hares, deliberately started to get us further and further away from the fact of what did happen on 22 November 1963.

HOOVERGATE

Let us consider the character of Oswald.

A loser. A failure at each job to which he turned his hand. No more successful in his marriage to Marina, the Russian he met when he was flirting with communism. His dissatisfaction with life had led him to travel widely, to Finland, London and Mexico.

This last fact was what set us on the road to discovering what lay behind the fatal shot fired from the Texas School Book Depository in Dallas on 22 November 1963.

It is beyond dispute that Oswald had taken a job at the Depository, shortly after arriving back from Mexico. A menial job, involving sweeping and cleaning. How he must have longed to escape from there, as dust from the shelves of tomes clogged his throat! But in the immediate future, it seemed all he could do to improve his lot was get a vacuum cleaner.

How do we know he did this? We can't, for sure. But the Warren Report states that on 21 November (one day before 22 November, it should be noted) Oswald was given a lift to his ex-wife's house by a co-worker – Buell Wesley Frazer, though his name is not important.

Oswald casually told Frazer he needed to pick up some curtain rods for his room. The next morning (22 November 1963) Frazer gave Oswald a lift back to Dallas. *Oswald was carrying a long bulky package, wrapped in brown paper.*

It is generally acknowledged that this was the rifle used to fire at President Kennedy, and that the 'curtain rods' story was an elaborate ruse. We agree . . . but think that the ruse was of an altogether different kind.

Suppose the package contained a vacuum cleaner.

But what would a twenty-four-year-old ex-Marine be doing trans-porting a Hoover from a suburb of Dallas back to the city? Obviously he wanted to borrow it for his job at the Book Depository. But he couldn't rely on a lift from Frazer every time he wanted to clean the floor – wouldn't it have been more economic simply to get another Hoover?

HOOVERGATE

By now our minds were spinning. When they'd stopped we tried to stand back and look objectively at the facts.

It is highly probable that Oswald spent time in 1963 trying to repair his broken marriage. One remedy he may have offered Marina was a trip to see her home town, Minsk. The only problem was: Oswald was too poor to afford their air fares. But what if a certain household name had a special offer of free plane tickets in return for the purchase of one of their products? This is just the sort of something-for-nothing scam the mentally deficient (a substandard IQ of 118, according to his service record) Oswald would have fallen for. He bought the Hoover and gave it to Marina, privately vowing to quit his job and stay put in Russia once they'd arrived there.

Oswald's movements in that first three weeks of November are shrouded in mystery, but it's a reasonable assumption that he merely carried out his duties at the Depository and awaited eagerly the arrival of his free tickets. Needless to say, he was in for another big disappointment. Such had been the demand that all he was offered was a round trip to Florida!

Something in Oswald must have snapped at that moment. This was the final slap in the face from the capitalist system that had betrayed him at every turn. For a while he entertained the idea of taking the plane then hi-jacking it and demanding that he and Marina be flown to Cuba. But she talked him out of it: what if the flight were full of other disgruntled ticket-holders, all brandishing guns and demanding to be taken to various world capitals? The result would be anarchy.

At least, Oswald reasoned, he could get his money back. Deciding to take his complaint to the top, he tried to contact the only prominent Hoover he'd heard of (a low IQ, remember).

Not surprisingly, the head of the FBI, J. Edgar, didn't return his calls – though they would have been logged.

By a stroke of the luck on which the wheel of history sometimes turns, Oswald learnt that the President was to visit Dallas at the end of that week. There could be little doubt that

HOOVERGATE

he would be accompanied by his top law enforcement officer. By now fairly crazed by the situation, Oswald resolved to confront Hoover with the physical evidence of the wreckage of his dreams. On the ride back from Marina's with Frazer and the wrapped vacuum cleaner, Oswald concocted the 'curtain rods' story, thinking that if Frazer was another thwarted customer, word might get round and Hoover would be besieged by angry nozzle-wavers. This was to be his moment, and his alone. How right he was.

But what persuaded J. Edgar Hoover to take the course of action he did? There is no evidence that he took a call from Oswald in the hours before the assassination (which merely means of course that it could have been erased from the record, a familiar FBI trick with unpalatable facts). But if our version of subsequent events is to hold water, there *must* have been a direct one-on-one phone conversation between the two men.

Surprised at being put through, Oswald probably blurted something out like 'You owe me money, you son-of-a-bitch.' At just the wrong moment his tongue must have let him down, and what he said came out as 'You owe me money, you – bitch.' A word guaranteed to terrify Hoover – it should be remembered that it has only recently come to light that the director of the FBI was a practising transvestite, and, as such, a prime target for blackmail.

Hoover reasoned correctly that the best way of protecting himself from a madman bent on revenge was to position himself in full view of the President's adoring public. Surely no harm could come to him in the motorcade? Accordingly he had a private word with the wife of the Governor of Texas, Nellie Connally. Initially she was reluctant to give up her seat in the limo, until Hoover hinted darkly that in his files was an allegation about Mrs Connally and some missing White House apostle spoons. She saw sense – an act that was to save her life.

Dressed in Mrs Connally's best bib and tucker, Hoover left the Ladies' Room at Dallas Airport observed only by Oswald,

HOOVERGATE

who had monitored his every move since Air Force One touched down. Outraged at the lengths to which somebody would go to avoid refunding a hundred bucks, Oswald decided to take the law into his own hands. He went straight to a downtown pawn-shop, hocked the vacuum cleaner and bought a 6.5 Mannlicher Carcano rifle before taking up position at his place of work – past which he knew the Presidential motorcade would travel.

The rest of the story has been told a million times, overlooking only one detail: what really happened. Oswald fired a shot at Hoover. Hoover was touching up his eyebrows at the time, and in his hand-mirror saw a glint of reflected light coming from the Depository's sixth-floor window. With a cry of 'Oh, my lipstick' he bent down to retrieve the imaginary cosmetic.

But not fast enough: the bullet hit the hair-slide at the back of his head, ricocheted and killed the President, *passing through the front of his head.*

HOOVERGATE

Needless to say this evidence was suppressed, by a past master at the game. Even the famous 8mm film taken by Abraham Zapruder was got at, after Hoover threatened to reveal the innocent cameraman as the director of the notorious *Arbuckle Snuff Movie* (cf. *Fattygate*, p85). Nevertheless, this is what we think the Zapruder Director's Cut would look like in this artist-enhanced enlargement of Frame 314.

INTERESTING FOOTNOTE
Could the President's life have been saved?

Much was made of the behaviour of the Presidential limo after the assassination, which lurched forward, careered from side to side of the road, depositing a Secret Service man unceremoniously on Elm Street, before taking the pretty route via the river and arriving at the Parkland Memorial Hospital five minutes after the motorcycle outriders.

COULD THE DRIVER HAVE BEEN A CLOSE RELATIVE?

A return to the Forbidden Planet?

From Grassy Knoll to Grassy Hole – set against the massive global consequences of the Kennedy 'assassination', a few symmetrical patterns flattened into the cornfields of England might seem like small beer. So we thought. Instead we seem to have stumbled on a possible explanation that could threaten the very future of Earth itself.

Not for the first time, on investigating the phenomenon we found that it was nothing new, and could well date back to the age of Chaucer. As is widely known, the 'Prologue' to his masterpiece *The Canterbury Tales* starts thus:

> 'Whan that Aprill with his shoures soote
> The droghte of March hath perced to the roote . . .
> . . . Whan Zephirus eek with his swete breeth
> Inspired hath in every holt and heeth
> The tendre croppes, and the yonge sonne
> Hath in the Ram his halfe cours y-ronne . . .'

But it will come as a surprise to many to hear that – such had been the success of the first volume – Chaucer was planning a sequel: *Canterbury Tales 2 – Back to Southwark*, when the returning pilgrims tell even more colourful stories. Unfortunately Chaucer fell out with his publishers, Caxton &

CROP CIRCLES GATE

Caxton, over the fee for the 'ecclesiastical rights', whereby the work would be serialized weekly and pinned up in church porches.

Literature was thus deprived of not only *Canterbury Tales 2* but also Chaucer's most ambitious project, when he planned to take his Pilgrims across to France in a rollicking narrative provisionally entitled *Toujours Lourdes*.

Only a fragment of the sequel to *The Canterbury Tales* remains, stored under electronically controlled temperature conditions in the Bodleian, and it was a privileged look at this which gave us our first inkling that corn circles had caused some excitement before:

> 'And so, tired but happy, the compaigny
> Of pilgrimes bade "Faren Wel" to Caunterbury
> And in the morwenyge torned their horses' heeden
> Homeward, or to whereen fansey leden
> Whan the sonne was heigh they stopped to take their ese
> At whych a churl whose tabard was with greesse
> Bishitten and whose face was fulliche spottes
> Cryed "I'll shewe ye somthinge far oute – see my croppes
> Looke how they have been flatted and how ronde
> The patroun is in whych they liggen on the grond."
> Wherto the Millere upped stikkes and stede he smoot
> And said, "Nexte thing yon Hodge wil charge a grote!"

And what are we to make of this entry in William Cobbett's travel classic *Rural Rides*, first published in 1830?

Thursley, Surrey – Thursday 7th August [1823]

The corn is not so forward here as under Portsdown Hill; but some farmers intend to begin reaping wheat in a few days. It is monstrous to suppose that the price of corn will not come down. It must come down, good weather or bad weather. If the weather be bad, it will be so much the worse for the farmer, as well as for the nation at large, and can be of no benefit to any human being but the Quakers, who must now

CROP CIRCLES GATE

be pretty busy, *measuring the crops all over the kingdom*. It will be recollected that, in the Report of the Agricultural Committee of 1821, it appeared, from the evidence of one HODGSON, a partner of CROPPER, BENSON and CO., Quakers, of Liverpool, that these Quakers sent a set of corn-guagers [*sic*] into the several counties, just before every harvest; that *these fellows stopped here and there, went into the fields, measured off square yards of wheat, clipped off the ears and carried them off.*
[Our italics.]

Were these 'corn-guagers' merely simple Liverpool Quakers? Or, when Cobbett had ridden rurally by, did they revert to their original plan, and continue measuring out corn *circles*?

Fast forward to September 1830, and the opening of the Manchester and Liverpool Railway. Guest of Honour: the Duke of Wellington. Also present: William Huskisson, the Member of Parliament for Liverpool and famous for his attempted reform of the Corn Laws, bringing down the price and making wheat more available to the hungry poor.

Some newspaper reports of the time also mention strange 'whey-faced wretches, their eye-glasses held together with vinegar and brown paper, standing at one end of the raised platform, each with pencil and jotting slate'.

Embryonic train-spotters, clearly. Or were they? After all, Stephenson's steam engine was such a new invention that there would be no need to number it – unless it was '1', which any fool could remember. Perhaps these spotty (in name and nature) creatures had some more sinister purpose in mind.

Every GCSE student knows what happened that day – the train entered the station and Huskisson stepped into its path and was killed. The repeal of the Corn Laws was set back twenty years and the wheatfields of England basked on, untroubled . . . <u>*apart from the outbreaks of circular flattening*</u>. [Our double-underlining.]

We find it incredible that Huskisson died as a result of a tragic accident. We think he had stumbled – fatally – on

CROP CIRCLES GATE

something involving his supposed Quaker constituent 'Hodgson', mentioned in Cobbett. Hodgson of course can be read as 'Son of Hodge' – the name referred to in the Chaucer fragment. 'Hodge' is thought to be a diminutive of name 'Roger', but over the centuries came to represent a general name for rough countrymen.

What if these 'Hodges' with their faces 'fulliche spottes' were not men of the soil at all – in fact, literally not of this earth? What if the similarity between the between the 'Green Man' of ancient country legend and the traditional 'Little Green Man' from outer space was more than a coincidence?

Convinced we were on to something, we set about researching all the outbreaks of crop circles in England in the late 1980s, and pin-pointing them on a map.

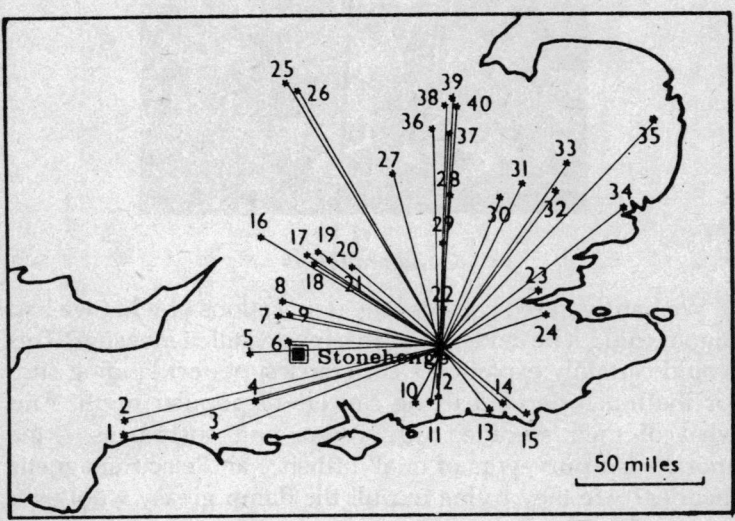

We hastened to the point bisected by these lines – the rolling chalk uplands of Surrey south of Guildford, sometimes known as 'the Devil's Salad Bowl'. To get a better view from the air we chartered a small plane at nearby Gatwick and circled the spot. The faintest of outlines was visible.

CROP CIRCLES GATE

To cut a long story short, we excavated the chalky hillside over several weeks. Here for the first time we can reveal the fruits of our labours:

Guildford Giant

We hardly dared consider the implications of what we had found: could it be evidence of an expected alien invasion? This would certainly explain the corn circles, perfect landing sites for the much derided flying saucers of popular myth. And what of their so-called discoverers and custodians – the anorak-clad purveyors of tidal influence and electromagnetic theories? Are they trying to pull the damp greasy wool over our eyes?

Could they be in reality the descendants of aliens, settled on Earth as an advance party centuries ago and biding their time until the moment is right for the full-scale invasion?

And if so, shouldn't they be humanely put down now, before it is too late?

Millergate

One of the enduring mysteries in the world of rock music concerns the album cover of The Beatles' Abbey Road.

Many ridiculous theories have been put forward as to the meaning (if any) of Paul McCartney walking barefooted across the zebra crossing. It always seemed absurd to us that this should have been regarded as a sign that he was dead. (Apparently it is a sign of mourning in Sicily to walk without shoes. So what?!) Of greater interest, we believed, was the object Paul was holding in his hand. At first glance it appeared to be a cigarette. But a closer inspection revealed it was in fact *a bamboo chopstick*!

What could this possibly mean? Only a detailed study of the lyrics of all the songs on the album would, we knew, help our investigation.

(At this point we should pay tribute to our neighbours, who so kindly put up with the repeated playing of *Abbey Road* at a loud volume for many days and nights with only a couple of complaints from a couple of them who failed (understandably perhaps) to appreciate the serious nature of our search for the truth.)

We were, of course, wise to the possibility of hidden messages in the songs which might only be discovered if listened to backwards (cf. *Brandenburg-Gate*, p73). Seven, maybe eight, times we span the disc in reverse, only to find complete gibberish. But then came the breakthrough! Late one night, in a tired, clumsy attempt to lift the stylus from the vinyl, it was dropped back on to the record *beyond the final track*. There – where there should have been nothing – was a clear, distinct sound. It was short and nearly unintelligible, but with sound enhancement it was found to be the one word, 'JAP'.

What could it mean? Was it a mistake or was this a genuine message? Enquiries were made at the Abbey Road studios and, once again, persistence paid off.

Maybe it was to get rid of us, or maybe it was fate playing a hand; either way, we were given permission by the studio's receptionist to browse through a pile of discarded tapes which she assured us were the out-takes from the *Abbey Road* recording sessions. We listened to every inch of it and, to be honest, much of it didn't sound like The Beatles at all. There was some big band material, some 1950s-type rock-and-roll, and even some country and western music. This was puzzling, to say the least.

It may be best to omit a recollection of the long days and nights of thought which went into the theory we came up with to explain *Abbey Road* (and so much more!). Instead, we shall let the theory speak for itself.

On 7th December 1941 the Japanese bombed Pearl Harbor and effectively joined the Second World War. Back in the Land of the Rising Sun, an entertainment corporation (which must remain nameless for fear of litigation, but which we shall call 'SAKI') saw the chance to expand across the globe and started to make plans for the future.

They had a vision of a world where every user of 'muzak' was supplied by SAKI. They would provide muzak of any description for use in every lift, reception-area and supermarket in every country. All they needed were the musicians to record it.

The senior executives began recruiting Kamikaze pilots who had completed their training but not yet flown on any missions. The high salaries promised to them (plus their limited prospects in the Japanese Air Force) made them easy targets for the SAKI headhunters and by 1943 they had a dozen pilots on their books.

The first task was to appoint a musical director who could compose and arrange the muzak. At that time there was only one man in the world up to the job – Glenn Miller. The SAKI pilots were briefed to kidnap him and bring him back to Japan. It was a difficult task, requiring months of preparation to gain access to a plane which was carrying the big-band leader. Indeed, the first attempt went badly wrong when a SAKI pilot mistook Leslie Howard for Glenn Miller, claiming 'they all looked the same to him'. (Howard was forced to spend the rest of his career tackling walk-on parts in Kabuki plays.)

After another year of preparation, a SAKI pilot managed to get behind the controls of the plane which was due to take Colonel Miller from England to France on 16th December 1944. Instead, he was flown to Tokyo (via Hawaii) where he was asked to head the muzak operation. Faced with the choice between a high salary as musical director or a living hell as bridge-builder and whistler, he took the job and began composing.

Over the years, musicians of every conceivable type were recruited and the output of muzak turned from a trickle into a flow. The favoured method of kidnapping remained by plane and the pilots took to simulating crashes which looked as though the musicians had died. Thus, in 1959, Buddy Holly,

Richie Valens and 'the Big Bopper' were flown to Tokyo at the same time as an identical plane was being crashed by a kamikaze pilot in North Dakota. On board that plane were three sad young men who thought they were on the way to the regional final of the Buddy Holly/Richie Valens/'Big Bopper' look-alike competition.

Patsy Cline took the SAKI yen in 1963 followed by Jim Reeves in 1965, Otis Redding in 1967 and half of Lynyrd Skynyrd in 1977.

By the mid-1960s, however, Glenn Miller was running out of ideas and energy. He was, after all, getting to be an old man. In 1967, SAKI decided to appoint a new musical director and their attention was drawn to the brilliant young composers, John Lennon and Paul McCartney. Their manager, Brian Epstein, was approached but he refused even to discuss the idea of his boys working in Japan at a time when the whole world was at their feet. SAKI reluctantly decided to remove Epstein from the scene and deal directly with Lennon and McCartney.

A SAKI assassin was dispatched to London and located Epstein's office. When a man who fitted (to the Japanese killer's eyes) Epstein's description appeared, he was followed home to Islington where he was brutally murdered by repeated hammer blows to the head. Tragically, the dead man was Joe Orton. The brilliant young playwright had been discussing with Epstein the film he was writing for The Beatles. When this was explained to the SAKI hit-man by a distraught Kenneth Halliwell, he too was murdered (poisoned with Nembutals) and framed to look like the killer.

Three weeks later, Brian Epstein was also poisoned and SAKI started negotiating with Lennon and McCartney. At first, both men were reluctant to discuss any kind of deal but when the beautiful Yoko Ono arrived and attempted to persuade them to think again everything changed.

Suddenly John Lennon was in love. He agreed to compose muzak for SAKI whilst continuing to work for The Beatles but declined to live in Japan. McCartney was furious and, over the next couple of years, tension between the song-writers began to mount. He did not tell anyone about the Japanese connection, however, since he did not wish to end up like Brian Epstein. But what he *did* do was to drop all the hints he could – maybe as a cry for help; maybe just as an act of defiance.

The references to Japan are there for all to see: in 1969 he married Linda *Eastman* and later that year came the *Abbey Road* album. McCartney's bare feet are a clear dig at the Japanese custom of removing one's shoes on entering a house and the bamboo chopstick in his right hand needs no explanation.

The break-up of The Beatles was inevitable after that point and Lennon concentrated more and more on composing muzak. He and Yoko Ono moved to New York where SAKI had opened an American headquarters. Their global domination of the muzak market was complete and they were searching for a new idea with which to expand their operations still further. In 1980 they invited McCartney to Tokyo to discuss such an idea. But, after nine days of intense negotiations (which were later explained away as a period of incarceration on suspicion of importing marijuana), he still refused to join their company.

Once more, SAKI realized they would have to turn to John Lennon for help. But they needed him in Tokyo to work full-time with the most senior executives on the new project (codename 'K'). In order to keep the project top secret, it was decided to smuggle Lennon out of America and, in December 1980, the 'assassination' outside his home in New York was simulated, allowing him to disappear without arousing suspicion.

Over the next ten years, the SAKI musicians worked non-stop to recreate the sounds of a thousand different pop groups, bands and orchestras. Cover versions of hundreds of the most popular songs in the world were recorded and packaged, ready for the launch of project K.

The result of that work is now all too plain to hear. In pubs, clubs and discos throughout this country – and soon all over the globe – SAKI's project K is dominating the world of entertainment. It is, of course, KARAOKE!

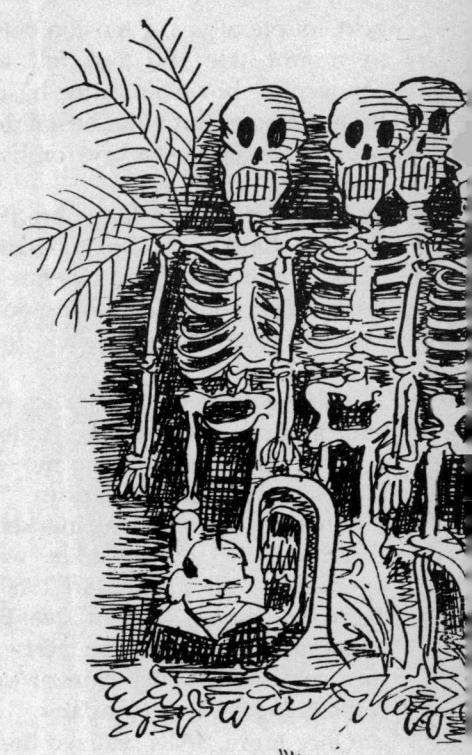

MILLERGATE

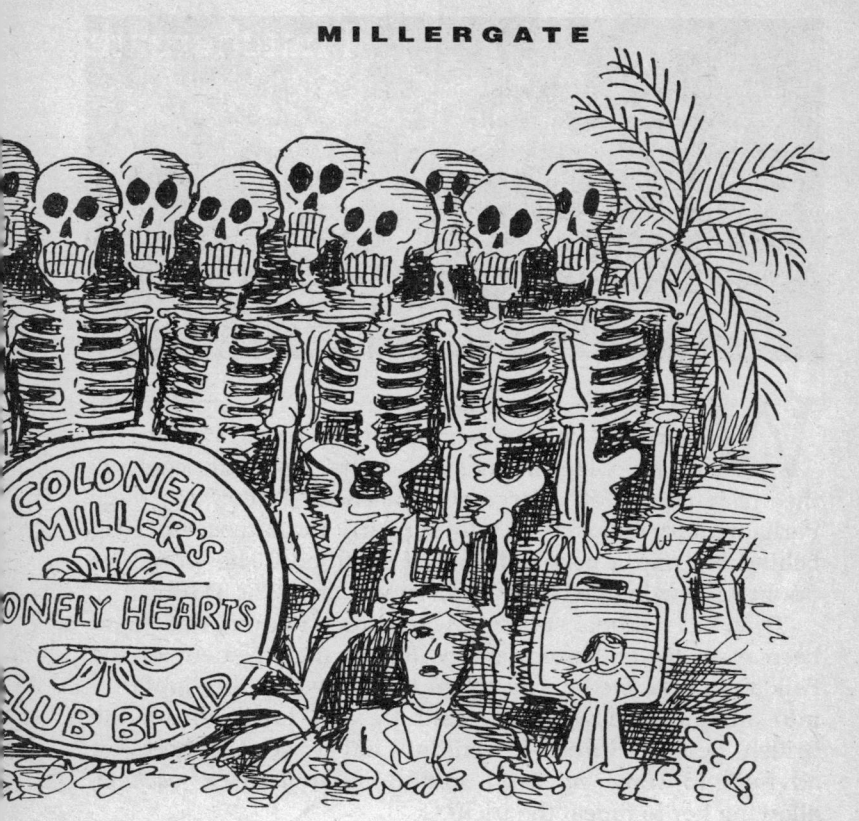

1. THE BIG BOPPER
2. PATSY CLINE
3. JIM REEVES
4. RICHIE VALENS
5–9. LYNYRD SKYNYRD
10. OTIS REDDING
11–14. GLENN MILLER BRASS SECTION

Thatchergate

With the jigsaw of history now falling rapidly into place, we felt we were ready to try and solve one of the biggest puzzles of the twentieth century: the resignation of Margaret Thatcher. With her huge Parliamentary majority, an adoring Party Conference not long behind her and a personal vote of confidence she would no doubt have won, the obvious question was: WHY THEN?

True, her national standing was at rock bottom, but it had been even lower before, and with her management of the Falklands War she had managed to parlay that unpopularity into an immense wave of gratitude and loyalty from the British people. Surely it couldn't have been beyond her advisers to come up with some similar *deus ex machina*, allowing her to repeat the trick?

Our investigations suggest that is exactly what was being planned.

We began by studying the date of her resignation closely.

22 November 1990.

The same date, as every schoolboy appearing on *Blockbusters* has written on the back of his hand, as the assassination of President John F. Kennedy – probably the last charismatic world leader before Mrs Thatcher. Of course, as we have demonstrated earlier, the shooting of JFK was a tragic accident

THATCHERGATE

(cf. *Hoovergate*, p112). This was intentional. There were other dissimilarities – Thatcher happened after breakfast in the Chinese Year of the Horse, JFK after lunch in the Year of the Cat. We were confronted by a growing certainty that there must be some significance in the date itself.

22 November 1990 – 27 years to the day.

Our minds began to engage a different gear. $27 = 3 \times 3 \times 3$. The Holy Trinity – 'Three in One, One in Three'. Or to put it another way: 'We Are A Grandmother'. But surely, we boggled, not even Mrs Thatcher would have assumed omnipotence, literally the divine right to govern? We all know that the Church of England is the Tory Party at prayer, but vice versa? Come off it!

Yet consider this. In January 1982, when the Malvinas were but a glint in General Galtieri's eye, Mark Thatcher entered the Sahara Desert and stayed there for six days and six nights. What was he doing there? It is our contention that he was searching – not for the way home from the Paris–Dakar Rally, as is generally thought, but for evidence of something so potentially explosive that the entire New Testament would have to go through another draft.

Did he find it? Perhaps a clue is contained in the press conference Mark Thatcher gave when he himself had been 'found' in the desert, after the alleged involvement of the Algerian army (have they ever been heard of since?). 'All I need is a beer and a sandwich, a bath and a shave' he said. 'A beer and a sandwich', for such a noted *bon viveur*? In any case, that combination was indelibly linked with trade unionists' visits to 10 Downing Street, which had famously ceased to happen after Mrs Thatcher's arrival there in 1979.

Could it be that 'beer and sandwich' was a codeword or phrase to reassure his mother watching on television, repeated via 'bath and shave' to ensure she didn't miss the point?

B...S...B...S

You didn't have to be Professor Alan 'Enigma' Turing to realize that these letters stood for their numbers in the

THATCHERGATE

alphabet, 2 and 19. But to what did these numbers refer? Something in the Bible, perhaps? Chapter 2, verse 19? Naturally we were about to turn to the Gospel according to *Mark*. But then we thought this is just what we'd be expected to do. So we looked again, in the Gospel According to John – the name, be it remembered, of Mrs Thatcher's successor as Prime Minister (cf. *Startingate*, p137). This is what we found in chapter 2, verse 19:

> 'Jesus answered and said unto them:
> "Destroy this temple, and in three days I will raise it up."'

The Temple. Spiritual home of the Knights Templar and their secular descendants: THE FREEMASONS.

It seemed clear that Mark Thatcher was warning his mother of the power of the masonic brethren in the land – cut off a limb, and it'll grow back immediately, stronger than ever. A timely reminder of the threat to her from disaffected members of her all-male Cabinet, many of whom were no doubt familiar with the apron and the funny handshake. Luckily the Falklands War came along in time to save her, and Mark's detective work had been in vain.

At this point we must acknowledge that we have drawn freely on the pioneering work of others. It would be invidious to mention their book – nor would they wish it. Suffice it to say that their researches (also, significantly, first published in 1982) add up to a compelling argument that we touched on both in our Introduction and *Gardengate* (cf. p28).

> *Jesus Christ was a family man whose sons and*
> *heirs lived on in Europe.*

The identity of His descendants was kept secret, vouchsafed only to the so-called 'Grand Master of the Prieure of Sion', the Parisian dynasty whose ranks include some of the greatest artistic and scientific geniuses in history: Leonardo da Vinci, Victor Hugo, Debussy (cf. *Brandenburg-Gate*, p73), Jean

THATCHERGATE

Cocteau . . . and Isaac Newton, the famous scientist, a native of Grantham, Lincolnshire.

Naturally, a bell rang in our minds, and this is where we started to get inklings of what really might have led up to that momentous event on 22 November 1990. It is well known that Mrs Thatcher's father, Alderman Alfred Roberts, was active in *Grantham* business circles, being among other things a Rotarian. It is inconceivable that he didn't also belong to the local masonic lodge.

Naturally enough, Mrs Thatcher had no time for such men's cliques. Indeed it is reasonable to suppose that, when making her famous remark 'There is no such thing as society', she was being especially vehement because of the *secret* societies that were hedging her about. And were not the original stonemasons' guilds the precursors of the hated trade union movement that she had done so much to stamp out?

On the night of the fateful first-round vote of Conservative MPs that November, Mrs Thatcher was in Paris – home, as we have seen, of the 'Prieures of Sion'. On hearing she had only defeated Michael Heseltine by about 50 votes, she announced: 'We fight on.'

The scene is remembered because of her dramatic appearance when Bernard Ingham ushered her down the steps, asking 'Where's the microphone?' An alleged BBC reporter pushed his way to the front with the words 'This is the microphone', and thrust it under Mrs Thatcher's nose.

What if it wasn't a microphone, but the ceremonial hilt of an ancient Templar sword, the presentation of which indicated that the recipient was being offered the next Grand Mastership?

Picture Mrs Thatcher's dilemma. To have accepted would be to embrace everything that was anathema to her: music, the arts and the teachings of Jesus – arch-exponent of the theory that there *was* such a thing as society, and what's more we were all responsible for each other's welfare.

She bit the bullet and resigned. This time, there really was 'no alternative'. The date she chose was a coded two-fingered (or rather three) gesture to her enemies, insisting that as far

THATCHERGATE

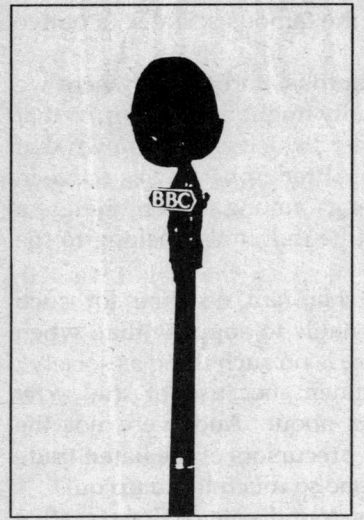 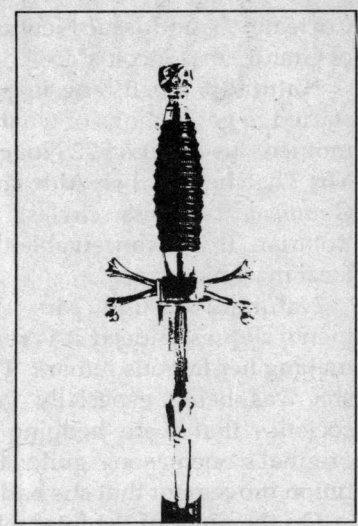

as she was concerned she was still, in short, God. But it was a last, feeble gesture: the Iron Lady had buckled under the pressure of the Lodge.

CONCLUSIONS

So many mysteries solved and secrets uncovered . . . yet we still weren't satisfied. It seemed there was something big swimming around, just beyond the visual range of our investigative bathysphere. A secret society perhaps, asserting its grip over history by dictating the way it wanted things to happen – not necessarily the way they should have turned out, much less how they were portrayed in the 'official' records.

Naturally enough we thought first of the Knights Templar, who are generally assumed to be behind any given conspiracy. But they ruled themselves out by not being in existence before the twelfth century at the earliest – in terms of the scale of our discoveries, only yesterday evening (or tomorrow afternoon, cf. *Hawking-Gate*, p5).

Time was getting short. Not only was the book due in, but news arrived from the Cumbrian coast of England that yet another chalk 'Giant' had been excavated, near the Sellafield nuclear plant.

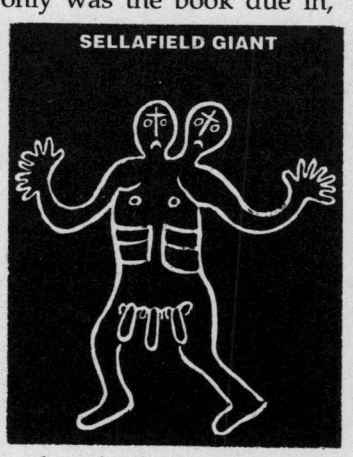

It seemed to prove our original hypothesis correct, that history *was* repeating itself. Clearly there was not a moment to lose if catastrophe were to be avoided – we simply *had* to identify the sinister forces at work, manipulating the world's every move!

Our answer came in the most banal of circumstances: watching television on 3 April 1993. Yet it is somehow poetic that this most shattering of conclusions could have only one name. . .

STARTING-GATE

Suddenly all the fragments of our tentative interpretations flew together to form the most perfect mosaic. Questions which we had glossed over – only to have them nag away at us in the middle of the night – were suddenly answered, such as (in no particular order):

* Who turned a blind eye when Lee Harvey Oswald carried a rifle into the Book Depository?

* Who stopped the crowds invading the Garden of Gethsemane and seeing the substitute Jesus?

* Who let the camera crew into the next room to Fatty Arbuckle's?

* Why wasn't Moses allowed to cross the Red Sea?

* How was so much gunpowder smuggled into Parliament undetected?

* What was Emily Davison doing up at Tattenham Corner, instead of being allowed into the racecourse stands?

This last mystery should have given us the clue to the others. But it wasn't until we settled down to watch the 1993 Grand National that it all began to fall into place.

As every public schoolboy with an exeat to the local bookies knows, this was The Race That Never Was – a confusion of starting and recall flags meant that the Grand National had to be cancelled, at a cost of £75 million in void bets and a priceless blow to the nation's prestige.

STARTING-GATE

What if this was no accident? What if it was an assertion of power by one of society's Great Unsung, acting in the best – or worst – traditions of his bowler-hatted predecessors through the ages? Could there possibly be a freemasonry of officialdom, whose very existence had hitherto eluded us? This sporting print, glimpsed on an edition of the *Antiques Roadshow* and too quickly pronounced worthless, convinced us that we were on the right track:

STARTING-GATE

It was time to widen the horizons of supposition. We remembered the famous wartime Christmas Message of King George VI in 1939, which concluded:

> 'I said to the man who stood at the Gate of the Year, "Give me a light that I may tread safely into the unknown."'

The war lasted another six years, so it is more than probable that the reply was the equivalent of 'Sorry mate, I was just knocking off.'

The more we thought about it the more obvious it became that the progress of history had been impeded at every turn by 'Gate-men' whose motto is 'Thou Shalt Not Pass' – and it goes back to the dawn of time, as this painting recently discovered

in a cave in the Massif Central district of France would seem to demonstrate:

The First Jurassic Car Park?

By now we were cooking with gas. Could the phenomenon of the ubiquitous one-armed commissionaire in fact be an echo of Napoleon's famous pose with one hand inside his tunic – a masonic sign indicating little dictators everywhere? Or could their arms be *deliberately pinned* inside their bemedalled jackets, lest when they were released they went into Hitler-salute mode?

Was this, indeed, the *real* reason behind the widespread use of the term 'Gate' by journalists – who, after all, are in the habit of trying to force their way through closed doors? Are they the first to realize that these 'Gate-men' constitute the most dangerous of all secret societies . . . and are passing on to each other a kind of coded warning?

But these must remain tentative conclusions. It is for others to pick up the baton and uncover further evidence to confirm or deny our theory. To go further at this stage, we feel, might endanger our lives. We are content to have alerted the public via the medium of *GATE GATE*.

Or should we have entitled it

THE BOOK OF JOBSWORTH?